*ten*minute
stress buster

*ten*minute
stress buster

Jennie Harding

p

This is a Parragon Book
This edition published in 2004

Parragon, Queen Street House,
4 Queen Street, Bath BA1 1HE, United Kingdom

ISBN:1-40544-317-0

Printed in Indonesia

Produced by the Bridgewater Book Company Ltd

Photographer: Mike Hemsley at Walter Gardiner

Contents

Introduction

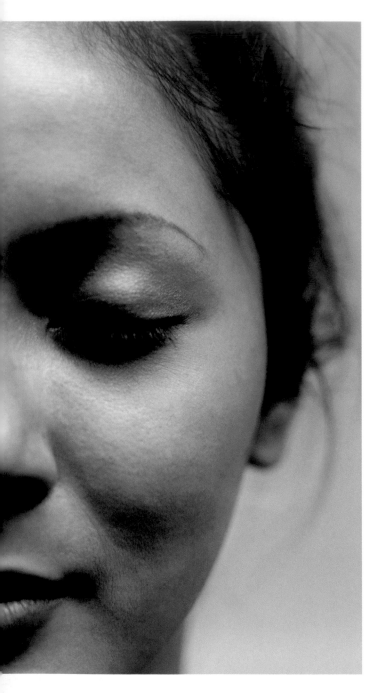

Welcome to *ten-minute stress buster* – the absolute antidote to the stresses and strains of modern living. This book is full of simple exercises and tools that you can use every day, easily and enjoyably, to take the pressure off your daily life. If you think you are too busy to relax, think again – all the stress-beating ideas in this book can be done in just ten minutes! These tips can be fitted in at work, at home, in the car or while travelling, and you will discover how to make your ten-minute 'time out' periods really worthwhile.

We live in times of incredible change, where the pace of life places ever more burdens on us. With so many things to do, so much to take care of, it is very easy to let life run away with us. We may find our time is filled with so many tasks that the effects of stress on our bodies, minds and emotions go largely unnoticed ... that is, until something goes wrong. Our bodies are very good at telling us what is going on, but perhaps we have forgotten how to read the constant signals before a problem kicks in.

The human body is an incredible, interactive vehicle, and it needs careful nurturing to keep it in peak condition. Exercise is one important way to do just that, but so is observing and managing stress. By learning to de-stress and relax, you allow your body to rest and regenerate itself.

Close your eyes, breathe deeply and rhythmically, and feel your stress levels go right down.

Stress is one of the major lifestyle factors of our times. It can be physical, mental or emotional – or sometimes all three at once. Stress often arises because you ignore the persistent signals your body is giving you about your environment. For example, sitting in the wrong position at your desk for years on end may be putting severe physical stress on your neck and shoulders, creating pain, possibly migraines, affecting your concentration and your mental state. Simply adjusting that posture may have positive and dramatic results.

Learning to manage stress is mostly a matter of learning to be aware of the signs, interpreting them and doing something about them as soon as they arise. Ignoring a problem is not the answer; noticing it and learning how to deal with it is the way forward. Modern stress-management techniques concentrate on giving you ways to cope, and this is exactly what *ten-minute stress buster* is designed to do.

In this book we shall look at a few ways of understanding what stress is and how it affects us, and then explore some fun and creative ways to help ease the pressure. We will journey inside the body and outside into your environment and give you a whole new way of understanding yourself. Managing stress is exciting – it opens the way to new levels of life experience. Learn to take your ten-minute 'time-out' periods, and see the difference they make!

Taking time out in nature as often as you can really helps to relax both body and mind

Using your senses

Your senses – sight, touch, hearing, smell and taste – enable you to interact with your environment. Even as a tiny baby you are already reacting constantly to the world that is in contact with you – the smell of your mother's skin, the feel of objects, the sound of music, the taste of food, the sight of someone's face. All these things very soon become open to interpretation – you learn to differentiate between smiles and frowns, you learn to distinguish between sounds that soothe you and sounds that make you feel uneasy; perhaps one day you put a hand on something very hot and discover from the searing pain that this is really unpleasant. Through your interpretations you begin to shape your world and change your

behaviour. Your senses tell you what appeals to you and what does not. Roses smell astonishingly sweet, look beautiful – and feel prickly to touch. If your senses tell you mostly positive things, you will probably decide you still want these flowers.

As life goes on, you continue to interpret the events that take place through sensory information, which is the basis for all marketing. The modern world we live in plays to the senses in more and more ways to entice us. The average journey to work exposes the eyes to maybe a hundred advertising messages. We are flooded with images, sounds, tastes, smells. Yet, ironically, one important way to manage all this over-stimulation is to recover the active awareness of our own senses so that we interact with the world from our own choice, through our own powers of observation. Thus we no longer just passively receive sensory information, but actively view it and choose what helps us best. For example, instead of being upset and annoyed by noise, we can learn to create

Touch is one of the most powerful and simple ways to understand your world.

opportunities for quiet, and rest our ears. If we work in a place where we breathe only recycled air-conditioned air, we can ease our mind by inhaling the scents of nature. By using our senses positively, we can totally change how we feel and learn to relax more effectively.

This book will take you on a 'journey through the senses' that will surprise and fascinate you. The more you try the exercises, both alone and with your friends for fun, the more you will start to think about how you live, where you live and what really matters to you. It may encourage you to make simple, positive changes in your environment that will make a real contribution to your sense of relaxation and well-being. It will give you tools to use to de-stress yourself and improve your levels of energy.

So now – relax, and enjoy the journey!

Inhale the perfumes of flowers to soothe and calm your mind, so you feel peaceful.

1 WhatIsStress?

Stress is a state you get into because of the way you react

to outside influences, like noise, debts, relationships, work

worries, all of which are known as 'stressors'. You may find

your reaction to a stressor is mild at first; however, you start

to notice effects if the same stressor repeats itself constantly.

Your body always tries to re-establish a state of balance, but if

the situation keeps occurring you may, after a while, begin to

show physical reactions like muscular tension, or emotional

reactions such as feelings of anxiety. These are signs of stress.

We live surrounded by potential stressors; how we cope with

them determines our state of health. These influences will not

go away, so the only way to deal with them is to recognize

them and change the way that we react to them.

Stress a closer look at stress

Understanding how stress affects us is very important and helps us to see how we might learn to cope with it. Not all stress is bad for us – some life events do stimulate and excite us in a positive way. If we can revert from stimulation into relaxation and find our inner balance, all is well. However, if we constantly overreact and become overexcited, we may eventually find ourselves in difficulty. The following two charts show the difference between a healthy response to a stressor and a stress pattern that can lead to illness.

Healthy response

In this diagram, the left vertical line shows the two extreme states of stimulation and inertia (total inactivity); most of the time we live somewhere between the two. The graph, which runs towards the right of the chart, shows the sudden 'blip' of a stressor; this person shows a rise in stimulation and then a dip down towards relaxation as they cope well afterwards through sleep or rest, and then return to their normal state of balance.

Stress

This diagram starts from the same point, indicating a normal balance between inertia and hyperactivity, but here the person is showing repeated stimulation reactions to outside stressors; notice how too much stimulation makes the graph dip very low, showing burn-out. This person is not returning to a normal state of balance, and therefore has the potential to become ill as a result of stress.

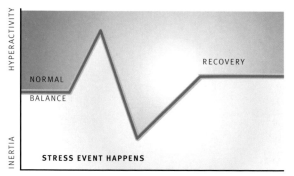

Finding balance between stimulation and relaxation is a healthy way to live your life.

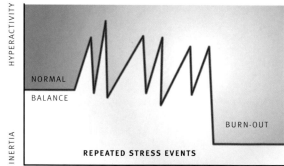

Repeated stress levels and no time for relaxation are pointers to ill health.

Why do we have these reactions? The answer lies in our genes. We still have bodies designed to cope with the lifestyle of our primitive ancestors, who relied on stimulation – the 'fight or flight' response – to deal with danger. However, we are exposed to stimulation of many different types in the modern world, so 'fight or flight' reactions in our bodies happen too frequently. If we do not allow enough time for recovery, we may well show signs of stress.

Many events in our lives can have a tremendously stressful effect. Here is a list of 13 of the most significant situations that can affect you, starting with the most extreme at the top, gradually decreasing as you work down the list.

Although pregnancy may be a very welcome event, it is also completely life-changing.

- Death of spouse or partner
- Divorce
- Menopause
- Separation from living partner
- Prison sentence or probation
- Death of close family member
- Serious illness or injury
- Loss of job
- Relationship difficulties
- Retirement
- Change in health of close family member
- Work more than 40 hours per week
- Pregnancy

If you have experienced one or more of these events over the last 12 months, then you may well now be suffering from signs of stress. Dr Hans Selye (1907–82), one of the pioneers of research into stress and its physiological consequences, said that '… stress is essentially reflected by the rate of all the wear and tear of life'. Notice how many of the 13 events in the chart represent times of major life change; retirement, for example, may throw the whole of a person's life into uncertainty – especially if they only identify themselves with their job. However, finding new directions or interests can transform this challenging situation into an exciting opportunity.

A closer look at stress

Stress getting in touch with stress

One of the most important ways of starting to identify how you respond to stress yourself is to get in touch with your own typical responses to it. We are all different, we have all had particular life experiences and been exposed to situations that are unique to us. We will all respond to outside influences in different ways.

Our reactions to things that stress us will be stored somewhere in the body; our physical self holds patterns or memories of stress. Dr Candace Pert from the USA has shown, through her amazing research into the brain, that 'mind' is not just in the head – all the different cells and tissues in the body are capable of holding emotional patterns. Yet because of the distraction of everyday external pressures, we are often totally unaware of the level of discomfort that we are actually holding.

Here is a ten-minute exercise to increase your own understanding of where you hold your tension – only when you have identified this will you be able to recognize it immediately and take action to overcome it. As the exercise needs you to be focused and aware, it may help you to make a tape recording of it to follow.

Learning to listen to the signals of your body helps you to identify your own stress patterns.

Inner scanning

Find a quiet place where you can sit undisturbed. Choose a comfortable chair and sit with a straight back, eyes closed, legs uncrossed, hands resting loosely in your lap. Take 3 slow deep breaths, and enjoy breathing out each time. Now focus your attention inside yourself and imagine you are taking a journey through your body. Keep breathing regularly, and start your journey at your head, then into your neck, shoulders, arms and hands, chest, abdomen, back, hips, legs and feet. Now – as you journey – where do you notice any tension? Is it in your shoulders, your back, your legs? You may well find at least one area, perhaps more. Make a mental note of where these sites are. When you have completed this 'inner scanning', take your awareness back to each area of tension you have found. When you are there, notice any sensations of discomfort or any emotions that arise. Try not to judge them, just observe them. Now breathe deeply and imagine you are sending deep warmth into the tension site, dissolving any negativity. Breathe this warm sensation into the area, and notice what happens. When you have visited all the areas you identified, breathe deeply again twice and stretch your fingers and toes before opening your eyes.

Don't worry if you feel you have not dissolved all the tension in one go – you may need to repeat this exercise a few times to start feeling a difference. The more you practise, the more you may begin to notice the typical locations in your body where you store stress. Getting to know where these areas are is really important – then you can choose the right tools to help you to relax them!

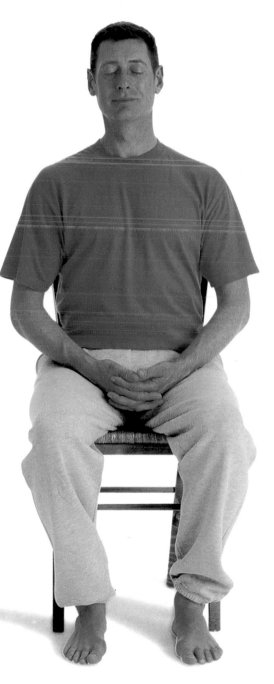

Make sure you sit in a position that is both comfortable and easy to maintain so that you can really relax.

Stress stress and immunity

One of the most immediate signs of over-stimulation and low levels of coping is a cold or 'flu – both of which are caused by a poorly functioning immune system. As the winter approaches and the days get shorter, your system may be reacting to lower levels of daylight and colder temperatures, but sustained levels of stress also affect the smooth function of your immune system – your body's own defence mechanism.

How? It's back to those cavemen again – whose physical bodies we still inhabit. When we react to an external stressor, we go into the 'fight or flight' response, as we have seen – primed to deal with danger. We are hyped-up to do something active like running or using muscles pumped full of blood to fight off an aggressor. At the same time our adrenal glands, which sit on top of our kidneys, are busy releasing chemicals into our bloodstream; one of these is cortisol, which actually weakens immune response.

This is not so serious if we are just experiencing an isolated stressful event, after which we can recover; however, if we remain in that hyped-up state over a prolonged period, cortisol continues to be released, the immune system protection is reduced and we are much more likely to contract an ailment such as a cold or 'flu. If you are the kind of person who seems to catch every bug going, you may need to look closely at the areas of your life that are causing you the most stress, and learn some ways to reduce or modify the effects.

Winter is a time when your immune system needs lots of support and you need to take care of yourself.

Immune boost using Eucalyptus essential oil

 10-MINUTE EXERCISE The quickest and easiest way to feel the benefits is to do a steam inhalation. Pour 2 litres (3½ pints) boiling water into a heatproof bowl. Add 4 drops Eucalyptus oil, lean over the bowl with your head under a towel, and inhale the aromatic steam for 10 minutes. You will immediately feel your breathing is easier and your mind is clearer.

You can also carry Eucalyptus oil with you – put 2 drops on a tissue and inhale the aroma any time you need to unblock your nose.

The wonderful antiseptic and cleansing properties of Eucalyptus essential oil are an immune-boosting gift from nature. The fresh, bracing aroma clears stuffy noses and heads, as well as lifting the spirits.

The good news is that nature has provided some very efficient ingredients to boost your immune system and give you extra support to help ease your symptoms. Eucalyptus is a huge and robust tree, mostly found in Australia, which can grow up to 100 m (300 feet) in height. It has highly aromatic leaves that release a powerful fragrance of essential oil when they are bruised. The leaves are distilled to obtain the oil in large quantities; it can then be used to unblock sinuses, ease head congestion and soothe coughs. The scent is also very effective at lifting your spirits, which are likely to be low when you're not feeling well!

Stress different types of stress

As a human being, you are made up of your body, your mind and your emotions. Your body takes you through the world, your mind interprets your experiences and your emotions are the feelings you receive as a result of events. Body, mind and emotions are all connected to each other and affect each other as well as working individually. Stress-related symptoms can surface in any of these three at any time; it is also true that often one area in particular dominates our reactions to stress.

The chart below shows these three different types of stress and their common symptoms, as well as suggestions for some very simple but highly effective coping mechanisms that may help to ease these symptoms. (Please note, however, that any symptom patterns that arise in a very persistent way should always be referred to a medical practitioner for advice and help.)

The ancient Yin-Yang symbol illustrates how energy flows.

Already you are able to see that it is useful to vary the approaches to managing stress, depending on what type it actually is. Physical symptoms are best managed through therapeutic and gentle touch, mental symptoms through visual activity, and emotional symptoms by establishing a peaceful space around you.

The Yin-Yang symbol is an ancient Chinese representation of

the three types of stress

type	symptoms	coping mechanisms
physical	High blood pressure, migraines, headaches	Massage, acupressure
mental	Poor concentration, negative thinking, lack of motivation	Eye exercises, meditation, creative visualization
emotional	Mood swings, anxiety, tearfulness	Time in nature, breathing exercises

the different life forces that flow through us at all times of our lives. Within the pale side of the circle is a dark dot, and within the dark side, a pale dot. This represents the constant shift of energy from active to passive, stimulated to calm, uplifted to low, and the two halves of the symbol are joined by a curving line, which suggests the flow of these states from one to another. Yang, representing an active, dynamic, outer flow, is not better than Yin, representing a passive, receptive, inner energy flow – both are needed to maintain balance. Both are needed for a full and vital life.

A vigorous walk in nature can help to ease physical and mental pressures.

The 10 breaths – Special breathing exercise for emotional stress

10-MINUTE EXERCISE This may not even take you 10 minutes! The next time you feel emotionally upset or angry, find a quiet corner somewhere, sit down and count 10 breaths – in and out equals one breath. They don't have to be big, deep breaths, just even and regular. What usually happens is that after about 6 or 7 you lose count … and you feel quite different. Your pulse rate slows down, your mind calms itself and your awareness comes back into your body. The problem may not have gone away, but you will be much better placed to deal with it. Try it!

Stress the senses and stress relief

The idea that touch, taste or smell can help to relieve stress may seem unusual, but in fact these are some of the most useful tools you possess. As we have already seen, the senses allow you to be in contact with your environment; by increasing and expanding how you use them, you can change how you perceive the world around you. In stressful situations, the right sensory tool can help you into a relaxed state, which allows you to cope.

Let's look at each of the senses and the effects they can have on stress.

Touch

Emotional feelings of distress, anger or anxiety often arise from loneliness or isolation. Touch, if given sensitively and with care, slows down the heart rate and creates a feeling of support. A hug, or simply a reassuring hand on the arm, instils a sense of security and relaxation from stress. The sense of isolation is lifted at once.

Taste

Many tastes, both good and bad, are actually linked to particular memories, often going far back to childhood. Certain flavours like vanilla are commonly perceived as 'comforting' – some researchers have suggested that this is a link to the taste and aroma of mother's milk, the original 'comfort food', linking to feelings of security.

Smell

The sense of smell is also very powerfully linked to memories and feelings, often causing remarkable responses. Natural aromas like lavender have a relaxing effect on many people; vaporizers with Lavender essential oil have been used to help people in hospital wards who have sleeping problems, reducing the need for sleeping tablets.

Sight

Colours have powerful effects on the eyes and the mind. Strong colours like bright red, orange and yellow are very stimulating; blues, greens and purples are much more soothing and calming to the vision. This is why natural scenes filled with greens and blues are instantly relaxing to look at, whether you are actually there or whether it is just an image.

The aroma of Lavender essential oil, distilled from the flowers, has a wonderfully calming effect on the mind.

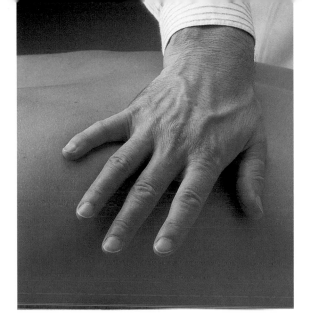

Gentle and sensitive touch brings about a feeling of peace and security, dissolving any fears or anxieties you may be experiencing.

Hearing

Noise is one of the biggest outside stressors of our time. Our ears are incredibly sensitive; listening to particular sound patterns – whether it's a pneumatic drill or classical music – actually alters the frequency of our brain waves, either towards a stress reaction or towards relaxation. Time spent listening to beneficial sound is an extremely effective way to de-stress.

Sound bath

Either on a good stereo or through headphones, sit back and listen – attentively – to a calming piece of music like the 'Largo' from the New World Symphony by Dvořák. Imagine that the sounds are literally bathing your ears. This is a simple and very effective end-of-day 'wind down' – notice how you feel afterwards.

Bathing your ears with beautiful music even for just a few minutes changes your brain-wave patterns and calms you down.

Stress sensory success with stress

Sensory approaches to stress are being used in many areas of the community. Psychological studies have shown that positive use of the senses is highly beneficial to the mind, helping to keep brain processes alert and maintaining mental, emotional and physical vitality. Bringing sensory awareness into working and living environments has lasting and noticeable effects on our feelings and attitudes. Here are some examples of areas where sensory approaches are helping many kinds of people.

In the workplace

Many work environments are full of harsh lighting, poor air quality and computer screens that glare into the eyes. Simple remedial techniques such as installing daylight simulation bulbs to emit a more soothing light to the eyes, using vaporizers with natural oils to improve the atmosphere or introducing living plants all bring changes to the space, improving people's concentration. Forward-thinking companies implementing such changes have noted improved performance in their workforce.

Growing old creatively

It is a fact that the population will soon be dominated by those over the age of 50, with life expectancy increasing well into the 90s and even beyond. Working to use and enhance the senses in older people is an approach to care in some residential facilities. Establishing sensory gardens full of plants that smell, look, feel and even

Encouraging sensory alertness in older people enhances their quality of life.

taste good encourages people to spend time outside. Activities like art, painting and sculpture as well as music and dancing keep social skills active and promote creativity. In care homes such as these it is not uncommon to find wonderfully active people with marvellously creative skills, which they are using and enjoying well into their advancing years.

Working with nature

Volunteer organizations like The British Trust for Conservation Volunteers encourage people of all ages to get out into their local countryside and experience it at first hand by taking on conservation work. As well as helping the local area, people find that their understanding and awareness of the way the natural world works is greatly enhanced. Time out in the fresh air is de-stressing in itself, and using touch, sight and other senses to interact with nature directly is immensely satisfying.

As human beings we are highly sensitive to the environments we inhabit. Modern living may have surrounded us with new technology and time-saving devices, yet it has also isolated us from the outside world that our senses are created to explore. The more we allow ourselves to open up to our senses again, the more we will be encouraged to enjoy the riches of our direct experiences. As you progress through this book, you will discover many ways to enjoy your own journey.

Use healthy, living plants to transform an office into a more supportive environment.

2 TheSensoryJourney

In this chapter we will explore each of the five senses in turn —

sight, taste, smell, touch and hearing. You will discover more

about how each sense works, then find ways to improve your

awareness of that sense and its ability to aid relaxation

and well-being. Some of the exercises in this section are practical,

others show you ways to de-stress. Everyone reacts differently to

outside influences; after a time of pressure, some people prefer

to slow down, while others enjoy the stimulation of a different

kind of activity. Both are beneficial, and both are available here

for you to choose what suits you best. It's a good idea to read

through all the sections in sequence, then choose one of the

senses that really appeals to you and explore that one first in

more depth. You may like to keep notes of your experiences so

that you have a personal record of what works for you.

Sight

Our eyes are the main way we actually interact with the world around us. They account for around 70% of our sensory perception. The eye itself acts very much like a camera; it has a curved lens, which becomes thinner in order to see something in the distance, or thickens to view something closer up. The iris, the coloured part, is actually a muscle that changes the size of the pupil – a small hole – to allow different amounts of light into the eye. The back of the eye (where the film is in a camera) is the retina, containing two types of light-sensitive cells called rods and cones. The rods help us see in darkness and show us black and white; the cones specialize in red, blue and green. The combined signals from these cells allow us to see the incredibly varied pictures of our world.

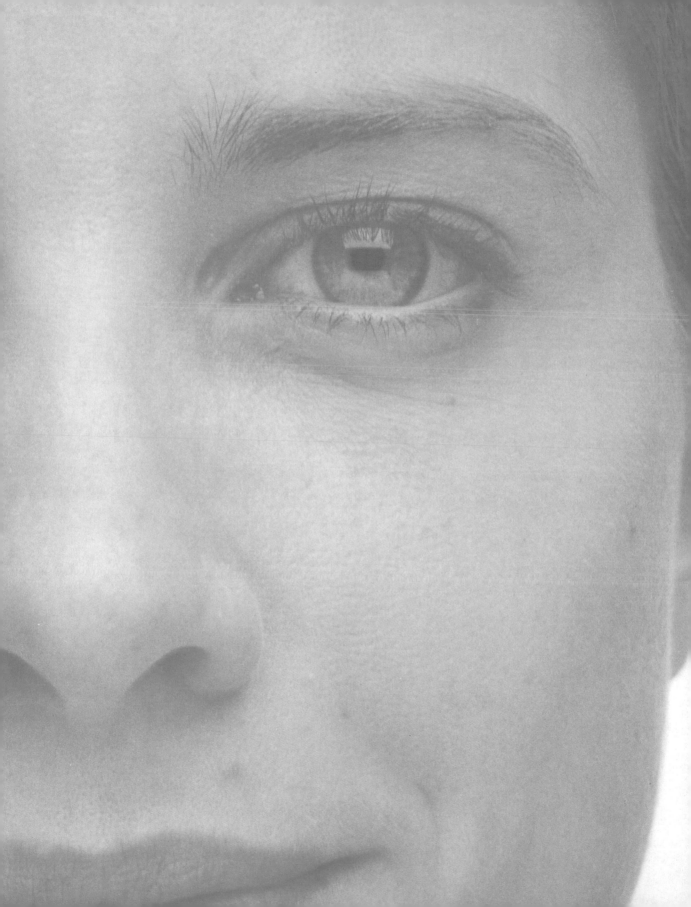

sight a rainbow of colours

The colours visible to the human eye form what is called the 'spectrum' – red, orange, yellow, green, blue, indigo and violet. These colours in all their variations attract our attention and have a strong influence on how we feel. The colour chart opposite shows the seven colours of the spectrum, some of their muted shades, and their effects on mood. Black and white are included at the end – black absorbs all colours, and if you make a colour wheel of the spectrum and spin it fast enough, they merge to become white.

Modern fashion in decorating tends to use muted shades of colours in living space, as opposed to the primaries. This is because muted shades feel more restful to the eye. Bolder shades work in different surroundings, where there is a lot of dynamic activity. In nature, flowers with brilliant colours, like reds and yellows, look balanced by their green leaves, and the contrast attracts insects. Incidentally, research shows that insects can see colours beyond the human eye, into the spectrum called ultraviolet; in this light, flowers look like helicopter landing pads directing the insects to land.

The vibrant, brilliant colours of flowers are instantly attractive to our eyes.

the spectrum of colours

primary shade	muted shades	effects
red	pinks	warming, stimulating, dynamic, powerful (pink is calming)
orange	salmon, apricot	warming, cheering, positive, outgoing
yellow	lemon, gold	opening, brightening, expansive, clarifying
green	lime, olive	soothing, calming, refreshing, restful
blue	pale blues, turquoise	gentle, cooling, soothing, peaceful
indigo	dark blues	relaxing, calming, deep, restoring
violet	lilac, purple	cooling, mentally expansive, restful
black	greys	enveloping, slow, contracting
white		brilliant, cold, expansive

Colour visualization

10-MINUTE EXERCISE You may wish to tape this exercise, pausing at the end of each phrase to allow time to create the images in your thoughts.

Imagine you are walking outside on a very warm day. There is a breeze blowing, you feel very calm. As you walk, you see a bush of deep red roses, with petals in rich crimson shades. You continue, and then your eye is attracted to a patch of bright orange marigolds, raising their faces to the sun; then a glorious golden sunflower. As you walk, you see a clump of trees, heavy with rich green leaves, swaying in the wind. After that, a patch of bluebells in spring; then the deep blue of delphiniums, tall summer flowers. Finally, you stop in front of a field of lavender, tiny violet blooms stretching away as far as you can see. Relax and enjoy these colour sensations, then slowly stretch your fingers and toes to wake up.

Use the 'colour visualization' exercise to imagine the rich and varied colours of nature.

A rainbow of colours   29

sight colour in your environment

What is your environment? You may relate that idea to your home, maybe your place of work, or the area where you live. You spend virtually all your time in these places, yet perhaps you have never sat down and observed what kind of colours are around you. You may well spend more time at work than at home, so the environment there will be having a strong effect on your vision.

If, like many people, you work in an office environment where white walls, grey carpets and fluorescent lighting are the norm, and spend your time staring into a computer, then the visual information your brain is receiving will not be varied. This accounts for feelings of boredom and frustration in the space. In Scandinavia, there are examples of large corporations like banks where efforts have been made to introduce living plants, flowing water, and colour schemes from nature, such as soft greens and golds, in order to make the work environment pleasant and supportive to staff. You may not have any say in how your workplace is designed, but perhaps you can introduce a few coloured items into your own area – a plant, a favourite picture, things you can look at to rest your eyes.

In your home, you do have control over your space. There, use of particular shades will affect your mood – soft greens to soothe, warm apricot shades to give a feeling of comfort, fresh yellows to uplift you. Your home is a place that should nurture you and give you sanctuary, where you return to be refreshed and renewed. Have you thought about your space like this? Try the exercise opposite for ten minutes and think about the results. It may be time to redecorate!

Many offices are full of harsh light and little colour, which can adversely affect both your concentration and your mood.

Colour assessment

10-MINUTE EXERCISE Take a walk around your living space and note down all the colours you have used to decorate it. Compare those colours to the chart on the previous pages, especially to the notes about effects on mood. Think about how you feel in your space, and how you would like to feel. Is your sleeping space decorated in a restful way? How is your kitchen? Your sitting room? Relating to colours in terms of how they make you feel may be new to you. Notice the balance of colours in your space, and think about any particular lifestyle issues you may have. For example, if your bedroom is bright red and you are having trouble sleeping, it may be time to change the colour scheme to more soothing shades.

Your home should be a comforting and pleasant space for you to come home to and enjoy.

sight eye-care exercises

The eye itself is made up of a series of intricately connected muscles. These are constantly contracting and expanding, allowing light in or reducing glare so that you are comfortable, and turning so that your eye can move to enable you to see from side to side or up and down. Like any muscles in the body, these need exercise to keep them healthy. Most of the time we are looking ahead, and rarely use the eye muscles to their full capacity.

Here are two exercises for the eye, which are very simple to do and come from the tradition of yoga. They are particularly recommended if you spend a lot of time at a computer. They are relaxing to do at any time, particularly in the evening. Each exercise takes ten minutes; you can do them one after the other if you wish, or just one at a time. If you wear glasses or contact lenses, remove them before you start. Remember – if you experience any problems with your vision, you should see a medical practitioner or an optician as soon as possible.

Eye movement

 Sit in a comfortable chair, relax, close your eyes for a moment and take a few gentle, even breaths. Now open your eyes and, keeping your head perfectly still, look up as far as you can for 5 seconds. Don't strain, just feel the movement. Now do the same thing looking down. Now look straight to the right without turning your head, then to the left, each time for 5 seconds. Close your eyes again and relax for a minute. Now open them, look up in a right diagonal direction for 5 seconds, then up in a left diagonal direction. Next, look down in a right diagonal direction, then down in a left diagonal direction. Close the eyes again for a minute and rest. Finally, open them again, and starting with straight up, move your eyes around all the positions in a circular direction, for 2 seconds in each position, first to the right – right up diagonal, straight right, right down diagonal, straight down, left

32

down diagonal, straight left, left up diagonal, and back to the beginning. Then do the same thing to the left, in a circular direction. Then rest, and relax.

Eye focus

10-MINUTE EXERCISE For this exercise you need to light a candle, place it on a table in front of you, and dim any surrounding light. The gentle warm yellow tones are soothing, with no glare. Sit comfortably and just focus your attention on the candle flame. Watch it carefully, noticing how it contains many colours, even tinges of blue; see the glow that actually surrounds the flame itself. This is a kind of meditation, which quickly calms the mind and helps you to slow down and relax at the end of a long day.

Eye exercises take a little practice but, if done regularly, really help tone your vision.

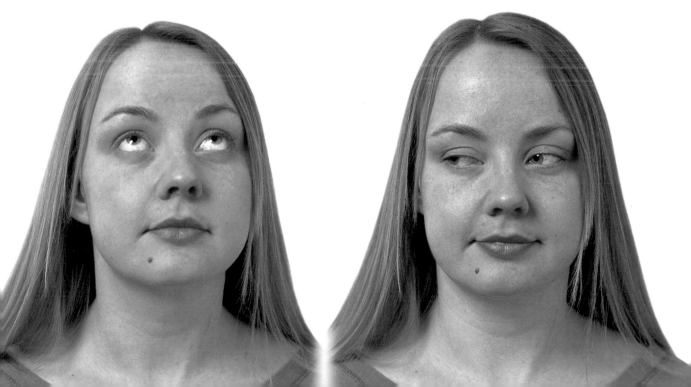

sight looking after your eyes

It's important to take care of your eyes; as well as regular eye checks, there are also some very simple things you can do, some in less than ten minutes, which give your eyes the chance to rest and recuperate. One or two of these ideas can be done anywhere – even at your desk, for example. It is a good idea to follow these tips to keep your eyes comfortable through your working day. Obviously it is best if you can do these eye-care activities for a full ten minutes at a time, but even just a few minutes will help. Remove your glasses or contact lenses before beginning.

Palming

Rub the palms of your hands together very briskly, until you feel a build-up of heat and a tingling sensation. Then simply place your palms gently over your eyes. You can choose to keep them open or closed, as you prefer; you should be able to feel your warm and tingling hands soothing your eyes. Relax for a moment or two. Repeat the palming 3 times.

Simple eye acupressure

The eye socket is the bony part of the skull that surrounds the eye. There are many points in this area that link to meridians, lines of energy that pass through the body and all its organs. Acupressure means applying pressure to these points with the fingers. When you apply pressure here, it is very important not to stick your fingers into the eye, or dig in too deeply in the

Palming is a quick and simple way to relax the eyes and ease mental stress.

delicate area underneath; keep your fingers in contact with the eye socket.

First, gently press upwards under the bony ridge from the outside of the eyebrow inwards, using the pads of your fingers. The points on either side of the bridge of the nose may be tender. Then, starting back at the outside corner of the eye, press downwards gently along the lower bony ridge of the eye socket. Some of the points you are stimulating also clear the sinuses. Repeat the upper and lower processes twice more.

These pressure points can ease the sinuses as well as helping to soothe the eyes. Make sure that you are gentle when you apply pressure.

Natural eye soothers

These are easy to do at home. One idea is simply to cut 2 slices of fresh cucumber from the fridge, and lie down comfortably, placing the slices over your eyes. Cucumber has a very high water content, which hydrates and soothes the eye area; within the plant tissues are ingredients that reduce redness and puffiness. Another option is to make a mug of camomile tea with 2 tea bags; allow the infusion to cool, then squeeze out the excess water and place the tea bags over your eyes. Camomile is a herb well known as an eye soother. The remaining infusion can be used as a lotion to bathe the eyes. Discard the bags and liquid immediately after use.

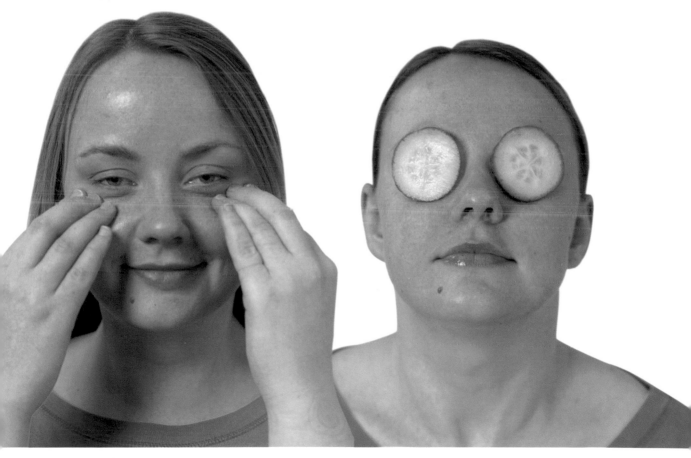

sight visions of nature

One of the reasons we love holiday brochures is the gorgeous photographs of sun-drenched scenes of nature. Being on holiday is associated with contact with nature, and the best hotel rooms have some kind of natural view – we are even prepared to pay extra for it. We anticipate the place we are going to with such excitement – probably because it represents such a contrast to what we normally see. This shows how much we value what our eyes perceive, and also how important it is to us to be in natural surroundings – because they are beautiful.

Fortunately, we do not have to go to the ends of the earth to see beauty. Very often it is right in front of us. Even if you don't have a garden or a balcony, you can enjoy plants in many ways. My grandmother lived in a terraced house with a simple, tiny back yard; in it she had a single enormous hydrangea bush. She fed it with natural compost – tea leaves and all the peelings from her kitchen – and it grew higher than the wall. Its enormous pink flowers and glossy green leaves gave her immense pleasure.

If you have the chance to get out into nature, let it move you. Become more observant of colours, shades, textures. Look at the perspective of distance, and contrast that to what you see close up. Let your eyes expand to take in a total view, then close them and see what you can remember of it. Bring your attention to something intricate, like a single flower with raindrops suspended inside like tiny pearls. Examine the colour, see how it changes, observe the shape and the

Let your eyes perceive beauty even when it is hidden away on the underside of a leaf.

astonishing geometry. Let your vision be a gateway to the quite extraordinary wonders of the natural world. If you have a garden, make a point of really observing it through all the seasons. Colours, textures and shapes are constantly changing, as sunlight angles move according to the time of year and plants move through their growth cycles.

Seeing – vision – is all about light, and the effects it has on everything around us. Remember, too, that our eyes can see very well in the dark – and if you have the

Stunning natural landscapes, such as this glorious mountain scene, are an inspirational feast to the eyes.

chance, go out and really look at a clear night sky. If you are far enough from city lights, the pattern of stars is extraordinary, and even the silken swathe of the Milky Way can be seen. Street lamps are a new phenomenon. For thousands of years we have relied on the stars and moon to light our way, and our eyes to navigate. Beauty is in the eye of the beholder.

Visions of nature   **37**

Taste

We need to eat to survive, but we also like to enjoy it. Over the millennia of our evolution, we have grown to like countless flavours and textures in our food. The tongue is the main physical structure linked to taste; a smooth pad covered with tiny 'taste buds' scattered over the surface. We can distinguish sweet, sour, bitter and salty tastes in the mouth itself; the textures of food are picked up by thousands of tiny nerve endings in the tongue, which can detect minute differences in feel such as a tiny bone in a mouthful of fish. Yet there is a lot more to taste than the tongue. The complex experience of flavour is also down to the sense of smell – as much as 80% of our sense of taste comes through the nose. Think about that the next time you pay for an expensive meal!

Taste tastes of history and tradition

In these times of health-conscious eating and diets, it is perhaps surprising to discover how much the sense of taste has always been celebrated, even worshipped, in countless cultures across the globe. Food has always been used to make statements about power and wealth on a grand scale by kings and rulers; but even those of more simple status make efforts to feast at important life events. We still eat particular foods, linked to our individual cultures, to celebrate religious festivals and the key times of life like births and marriages. Taste is a way to celebrate the abundance of the Earth.

To wealthy Romans, food was a source of voluptuous excitement; their famous banquets were elaborately designed to tickle the senses, and dining was a regular all-night pastime with hosts competing to outdo each other in the complexity and daring of their dishes.

It was customary to make your guests walk in through thick layers of rose petals on the floor, drape them with scented floral wreaths, have slaves wash their hands with scented water between courses and waft them with incense … all as an accompaniment to the meal itself.

These dinners must have been a totally overwhelming sensory experience of flavour, texture and aroma.

In contrast, ancient Egyptians believed the universe was the same shape as the onion, and swore oaths on the onion as we would on the Bible. They were a regular food for poor and wealthy alike, and were often eaten raw!

In the 16th century, the Spanish conqueror Hernán Cortez noticed the Aztec King Montezuma drinking cocoa flavoured with ground-up vanilla pods; these long black aromatic pods came back to Europe in sacks along with cocoa, and were considered as valuable as the gold, jewels and other plunder. Vanilla-scented chocolate drink became all the rage because it was considered to be an aphrodisiac. Four hundred years or so later, our appetite for chocolate is as vast as ever – it remains one of the most sensually pleasing foods.

At the court of King Henry VIII, the cooks in the vast kitchens at palaces like Hampton Court would labour to produce elaborate dishes to tempt the king's palate. A favourite was different sizes of game bird, from a swan to a lark, all slotted inside each other. Meat was surprisingly highly spiced, not just to disguise the well-hung flavour, but also as a left-over habit from medieval times – the crusaders brought the tradition of using spices into western Europe.

Food has always excited us, interested us and given us energy. This is as true now as ever. We bring our world literally into the body through the foods we taste.

The Romans were famous for their elaborate banquets, full of exotic tastes and aromas to thrill the senses.

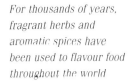

Chocolate comes from the cocoa bean, discovered in the New World and brought to Europe in the 16th century.

For thousands of years, fragrant herbs and aromatic spices have been used to flavour food throughout the world

Taste keeping an internal balance

The foods and drinks we consume have either acid- or alkaline-forming effects on our system. Acid and alkaline are opposing qualities, like two sides of a coin – both are needed, but in the right proportions. The average western diet is very high in acid-forming foods like meat and cereals, and very low in alkaline-forming foods like vegetables and fruits; this can be detrimental, leading to a build-up of toxins in your system which are hard to eliminate and can lead to health issues like stomach or kidney problems.

To understand the acid-alkaline relationship, look at the chart below. The pH value is a numerical way of showing the difference – the lower the number, the higher the acidity. Stomach acid is highly corrosive.

Alkaline-forming foods help to 'buffer' the effects of acid-forming foods, which is why we eat them together, like chicken (acid) and vegetables (alkaline). Also, dairy and soya products, in the right amounts, help to regulate acidity or alkalinity – we eat fruit (alkaline) with yogurt, bread (acid) with butter, or vegetables (alkaline) with tofu; these combinations are easier for the body to digest.

The average western diet tends to be 70–80% acid-forming foods and about 20% alkaline; in fact, this should really be more or less reversed. It is much more alkalinizing – that is, calming – to our digestive system to eat a larger proportion, approximately 70%, of alkaline-forming foods and a smaller amount, around 30%, of acid-forming foods. This still provides plenty of protein (found in meat, eggs, beans and pulses). Deep-breathing and relaxation alkalinizes or calms the system. High levels of physical activity and mental stress acidify or stimulate the system. Depending on your particular lifestyle, it is important to think about the types of food you are eating. For example, if you are stressed and consuming a high amount of acid-forming food, this can lead to over-acidity and high toxin levels; you need to try to eat a higher proportion of alkaline foods like fruits, salads and vegetables and drink more neutral water.

Balancing acid and alkaline foods helps support a healthy digestive system.

acid		neutral			alkaline
stomach acid pH1	wine pH3.5	water pH7	blood pH7.5	sea water pH8.1	baking soda pH12

effects of food groups on the body

acid-forming foods

sugar, honey, fats and oils, white flour, beans, wholegrains, cereals, red meat, fish, chicken, eggs

buffer foods

yogurt, cream, milk, butter, ice cream, cheeses, tofu

alkaline-forming foods

fruits, salads, green vegetables, potatoes, sea vegetables, salt

MEAT

CHEESE

POTATOES

EGGS

BUTTER

FISH

GREEN VEGETABLES

Alkaline-forming foods such as salads balance the acid-forming effects of proteins such as eggs and fish.

Food chart

 10-MINUTE EXERCISE Take a piece of paper and write down all the foods you have eaten in the last 48 hours. Also, list the activities you have done and how you felt mood-wise at the end of each day. Compare this with the chart – how much acid- and alkaline-forming food are you eating? Consider your stress levels and perhaps try a few changes.

Taste ten-minute fruit boosts

Many of our foods these days are full of artificial ingredients and chemicals that blunt our taste buds. The extreme sweetness of saccharin, used to flavour many fizzy drinks, is potentially addictive. In France, where good-quality food has been appreciated for centuries, there is the tradition of eating a fresh-fruit sorbet, quite literally to 'clear the palate', in the middle of a meal; the flavour of fruit is cooling and soothing to the mouth. As well as being full of vitamins and minerals, which are highly beneficial to health, fruits are alkaline and help to balance the digestive system.

Mixing fruit with milk and yogurt makes tasty and nutritious drinks.

A burst of freshness

Here are some wonderful quick ideas for fruit boosts, packed with vitamins and nutrients and full of fresh, vital flavour. These are a quick way of increasing your fruit intake, they taste great, and they can easily be incorporated into your daily routine, maybe at breakfast or in the evening. To make them, you need an electric blender, which pulverizes the fruit and mixes it with other ingredients. All the recipes make one generous serving of approximately 230 ml/8 fl oz.

Mango and banana smoothie

Mangoes have delicious pale-orange flesh packed with vitamin C, as well as minerals like potassium and phosphorus. When you buy a mango, test it for ripeness by gently pressing the skin, which should give way under your fingers. Peel off the skin with a sharp knife, then carefully cut the flesh away from the stone in chunks. Bananas are a great instant source of energy as well as B group vitamins.

Into the blender put the flesh of 1 mango; 1 peeled banana cut into chunks; 50 ml/2 fl oz natural yogurt and 115 ml/4 fl oz milk. Put the lid on the blender and whizz up until smooth.

Peach and raspberry smoothie

Peaches are rich in B vitamins and beta-carotene as well as minerals like calcium and magnesium. Use ripe fruit with no bruises. Wash and cut in half and remove the stone, not the peel. Raspberries are rich in vitamin C; wash them before use.

Into the blender put 2 peaches, cut into chunks; 125 g/4 oz raspberries; 50 ml /2 fl oz natural yogurt and 115 ml/4 fl oz milk. Blend until smooth.

The fresh, succulent tastes and bright colours of fruits literally do make your mouth water!

Orange and strawberry milkshake

Oranges are a great source of vitamin C, and strawberries are full of beta-carotene and minerals like potassium; remember to wash them before use. Into the blender put the freshly squeezed juice of a large orange and 125 g/4 oz strawberries. Add 115 ml/4 fl oz/milk, and blend until smooth.

Vary the fruits according to what is in season – and what you enjoy!

Get creative with the fruit combinations you particularly enjoy – try whatever you fancy!

Taste eating patterns and stress

By now, perhaps you are beginning to realize that your internal balance depends on the ratio of acid and alkaline foods you eat, as well as your lifestyle patterns – including your levels of physical, mental and emotional stress. Different foods affect different moods; unfortunately, what we tend to reach for when we are down are things like chocolate or caffeine, which are not necessarily the best option, much as we love them. A holistic approach to diet means observing your mood patterns and eating foods that support your system, rather than aggravating or depleting it.

Opposite is a chart of moods, showing foods that deplete you further as well as those that build you up and rebalance you. It is based on principles of Chinese medicine, which revolve around the meridians – lines of energy that pass through the body and the organs. Moods are linked to energy deficiencies in particular meridians, and the right foods can help to rebalance the energy patterns. Having identified your mood, try and eat less of the things that deplete you and more of the things that build you up. The quick tips are simple ideas to try as remedies when you need something to pick you up in the moment.

It is also important to avoid eating when you are severely stressed or anxious. It is far more supportive to your system to calm yourself, either through a relaxation technique like the ten breaths exercise on page 19, or by taking a break, going outside – then returning to eat your meal. If you are stressed, your abdominal area will be tensed up, and this can affect the efficient function of your digestive system. Eating while watching angry or violent scenes on TV can upset your digestive balance; eating in a relaxed and calm atmosphere is a pleasure and supportive to your health. This may be why it was often the tradition in medieval monasteries to eat in silence!

Try not to eat if you are either very stressed or feeling angry – these states are not conducive to eating and can cause indigestion.

foods to combat negative moods and emotions

mood	reduce	increase	quick tip	meridians affected
depression and melancholy	sugar, dairy, wheat	beans, fish, meat, rice	a salt taste, like olive or anchovy	lung, large intestine
fear	as above, plus meat	brown rice, cooked vegetables	apple juice	kidney, adrenals
anger	fat, salt, cheese, meat	salads, fresh vegetables	bananas, apples	liver, gall bladder
anxiety	wheat, coffee, chocolate	salty foods, brown rice	olives, anchovies	heart, small intestine
worry	dairy, sugar, honey	wholegrains, cooked vegetables	wholewheat bread and butter	stomach, kidney

If you want to eat while watching TV, try and choose images that are not going to upset or distress you. Remember – these feelings can disrupt your digestion.

Taste medieval mood foods

The idea that food affects how you feel has a long history. In the 12th century, in Germany, Hildegard of Bingen was abbess of a large community of nuns. The amazing Hildegard wrote books full of sacred inspiration, musical pieces, and advice on women's health and on dietary matters. Hildegard believed, as medical practice confirmed in time, that foods helped to rebalance the different 'humours' of the body – blood, phlegm, black bile and yellow bile – which were seen as vital to health; she even went further than this by relating foods to particular illnesses, including stress.

Hildegard's soothing recipes

Here are three very simple recipes, based on Hildegard's ideas, that can be made quickly to soothe your digestion, particularly if you have been under severe emotional stress. They take slightly more than ten minutes to prepare, but not much longer, and will each make enough for one person.

This illustration of Hildegard with her scribe, Volmar, is from one of her manuscripts. Hildegard is receiving wisdom from heaven.

OATS

Roasted oat broth with parsley

Oats are firm favourites of Hildegard's, because they are so easy to digest. Modern research shows that oats slowly release energy into the body, which helps to build strength. Oatcakes or porridge are easy ways to eat them. Here is a recipe idea that soothes tender stomachs in adults and children.

Place a small saucepan over a medium heat. Pour in half a teacupful of oats and stir them in the warming pan until they literally 'roast' – they turn brown and start to smell nutty. Stir 5 g/1 teaspoon of butter into the oats, and add a small, finely chopped onion. Cook for about 3 minutes. Pour 115 ml/4 fl oz of water into the pan, bring to the boil, add a pinch of salt and pepper and simmer for 5 minutes. Just before serving, add 15 ml/1 tablespoon of finely chopped fresh parsley.

Simple vegetable soup

Cooked vegetables – simple onions, carrots and cabbage – were the staple diet of many people in the Middle Ages. Hildegard regarded cooked vegetables as being particularly easy on the digestion, especially after stress or illness.

Wash, peel and chop a small onion, a large carrot and 3 Savoy cabbage leaves into very small pieces. In a small saucepan set over a medium heat, put 5 ml/1 teaspoon of sunflower oil, stir in the onion and cook for 2 to 3 minutes. Stir in the carrot pieces next, cook for 2 minutes, then add the cabbage leaves. Pour in 115 ml/4fl oz of water, bring to the boil, add a pinch of salt and pepper and simmer for 10 minutes.

Stewed apples with cloves

To this day, apples still grow wonderfully sweet in the Rhineland area where Hildegard lived. She believed that cooking them made them more gentle on the system. The addition of cloves as a warming spice during cooking improves the flavour as well as stimulating the tastebuds.

Wash, peel and core 2 ripe dessert apples and chop them into small pieces. Place in a pan with 4 cloves, 5 ml/1 teaspoon of honey and 45 ml/3 tablespoons of water. Bring the mixture to the boil and simmer for 10 minutes. Remove the cloves, and serve.

CARROTS

CABBAGE

CLOVES

APPLE

Taste herbs and spices

For thousands of years, humans have been using fresh and dried leaves, seeds, roots and berries to add flavour to food. Many of the common herbs and spices are key ingredients in herbal medicine; their medicinal use tends to call for larger amounts than would be used in food flavouring. Yet cooking with these natural flavouring ingredients is very beneficial to our digestion. In India, for example, dishes of rice, beans, starchy vegetables and meat are supplemented with cloves, cumin, ginger, coriander or turmeric – all of which reduce intestinal gas and improve the absorption of the food.

Using herbs and spices can add a whole new dimension to cooking. As a general rule, only a pinch of a herb or spice is needed to begin with; over-seasoning will not taste good. Herbs tend to have a calming and soothing effect on your digestion; spices will warm you up, particularly during the winter months.

Two 10-minute winter pick-me-ups

Fresh ginger and lemon tea

In a mug, put 5 ml/1 teaspoon finely chopped fresh ginger root, a slice of fresh lemon and 5 ml/1 teaspoon honey. Fill the mug with boiling water, place a saucer on the top and leave for 5 minutes to infuse. Sip slowly and let the spicy, fruity flavours and aromas of the drink banish winter chills and lift your spirits.

Fresh thyme and honey tea

In a mug, put 3 sprigs of fresh thyme (rinsed under the tap first) and 1 teaspoon/5ml of honey. Fill the mug with boiling water, place a saucer on the top and leave to infuse for 5 minutes. Lift out the sprigs of herb with a spoon and sip slowly. This lovely aromatic and sweet infusion is very soothing to sore throats as well as refreshing to the mind.

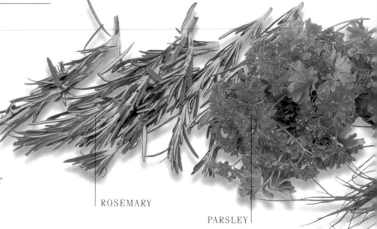

ROSEMARY

PARSLEY

CHIVES

Herbs – whether fresh or dried – add wonderful aromatic flavours to your cooking.

Spices are warming and mouth-watering, and stimulate healthy digestion.

CORIANDER   BASIL

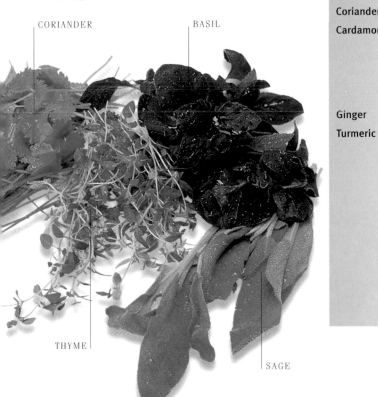

THYME

SAGE

beneficial herbs and spices

Here is a table of common herbs and spices with their benefits.

Herbs

Rosemary Marjoram Thyme Basil	These are all members of the family of Mediterranean herbs called the *Labiatae*; they stimulate gastric juices to help digestion and absorption.
Parsley Dill Fennel seed	These are all members of the plant family *Umbelliferae*; they help prevent stomach cramps and ease digestion of fatty foods.

Spices

Black pepper Cumin Coriander Cardamom	These are all seeds filled with highly aromatic oils. They come from the Far East and are used to ease intestinal gas and assist absorption of food by increasing production of digestive juices.
Ginger Turmeric	These two are aromatic roots that ease stomach cramps and have a warming, comforting effect that relieves indigestion.

Smell

Of all the senses, smell is perhaps the hardest to define. It has the power to change your mood instantly, even to stop you in your tracks – for example, passing a bakery and smelling fresh bread may distract you from your purpose and suddenly make you ravenously hungry! Your nose is smell's external passageway to the outside world; you inhale aromas through both nostrils. The microscopic aromatic particles pass up the nostrils to clusters of smell receptor cells like beds of microscopic sea anemones wafting in the back of your nose. The aromatic particles are trapped there and smell signals are triggered straight into your brain. Smells can immediately change how you feel, influencing your mood and behaviour – almost without you knowing!

smell smells and moods

The sense of smell still intrigues and often baffles researchers. It is known that the route by which smells travel to the brain centres is incredibly swift, with feelings or memories being triggered in less than two seconds. The smell of food instantly triggers saliva in the mouth and stimulates the production of digestive juices, making the tummy rumble in anticipation. The smell of a beautiful rose bush will direct our feet to the flowers, and perhaps like insects we will feel encouraged to bury our faces in the petals, overwhelmed by the sweetness of the aroma.

We all react to smells individually, according to our own life experience. Particular smells can trigger very powerful memories, often from far back in childhood. We find it very hard to describe smells individually – we tend to say 'that smells like …' or 'that reminds me of …'. This is because aromas trigger centres in the brain where our memories and feelings are stored. Babies and tiny infants relate to their world more through the sense of smell than any other. Smell is vital to life immediately after birth – babies use their sense of smell to track their way to the nipple.

As we grow, smells become associated with experiences. Take the smell of Christmas, for example – most people would associate it with a whiff of pine mixed with mandarin, complemented by a strong dash of clove or nutmeg and maybe a final touch of brandy and roast turkey. The smells of Christmas are a really important part of the festivities, creating anticipation and a sense of pleasure.

Aromas can have an immediately positive, uplifting effect on your mood.

Flowers, spices, seeds, fruits and leaves all have their own different, distinctive aromas. Rediscovering the smells of nature helps you to reconnect with your environment.

NUTMEG

CINNAMON

PINE CONES

Smells that make us feel good are likely to be triggering brain centres responsible for sending different chemicals into our system, such as endorphins, which give a sense of euphoria, or well-being. Aromas we do not like will often change our behaviour quite radically, making us move away or screw up our faces in disgust. Some smells make us feel relaxed and ready for sleep, others help us concentrate when we are driving because they stimulate the brain.

   The point is that we react almost without thinking. This is because smell is such a deeply instinctive sense, connected to the part of us that reacts through 'just knowing' rather than mental analysis.

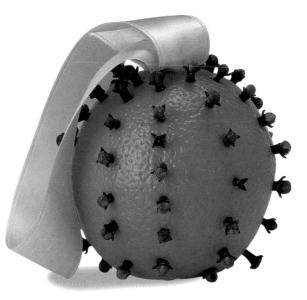

The smell of Christmas is a combination of evocative aromas such as orange and clove.

Smells and moods

smell aromatherapy for relaxation

Aromatherapy brings about a sense of physical and emotional well-being by using the natural aromas of selected essential oils, extracted from many different plants. Rose, lavender, rosemary, ginger, eucalyptus, lemon, cardamom and pine are just some examples. The essential oils in these plants can be used in a variety of simple ways in your everyday life, such as in baths, vaporizers and massage blends – their fragrances instantly uplift your mood.

Essential oils are found in flowers, leaves, woods, fruits, berries and roots; most of them are extracted by a process called distillation. Plant material is heated with steam, which lifts aromatic particles out of the plant fibres; the fragrant steam is cooled back to water, leaving the essential oil floating on top to be skimmed off. Fruits like oranges and lemons have essential oil in their peel; this is simply squeezed out.

Smell assessment

10-MINUTE EXERCISE Here is a fun thing to do when you buy a new essential oil. Simply put 2 drops on a tissue, sit somewhere quiet and inhale the aroma. Close your eyes and let yourself experience it. How does it make you feel? What does it remind you of? How would you describe this smell? Does it change over time? Learning how the aroma affects you will help you to use it in a way that suits you, and you may find that after ten minutes you feel quite different in yourself.

In summer, the lavender fields of Provence in southern France are a sea of purple and an ocean of fragrance!

Tuning in to your sense of smell can teach you a lot about your instincts and feelings.

essential oil safety tips

1 Never swallow essential oils.

2 Do not use more than the suggested numbers of drops.

3 Lavender and Tea Tree can be used neat on the skin (2 drops = 1 dose); all other oils must be diluted in a vegetable carrier oil for skin application.

4 Keep essential oils well closed and out of the reach of children.

5 If you are pregnant, consult a qualified aromatherapist regarding safe use of oils.

6 If you have sensitive skin, use half the stated drops in any blend.

7 Keep your eyes closed when inhaling scented steam.

8 For massage, use half the drops in any stated blend for children aged 2 to 10. Children over 10 can receive the full blend. For baby massage blends, see pages 86–87.

9 If you massage into the skin any blends containing Sweet Orange, Lemon or Mandarin oils, you must not expose the skin to strong UV light or a sunbed for 12 hours afterwards.

smell key essential oils

Here are six key essential oils for a simple aromatherapy starter kit. When you buy essential oils, make sure they come in dark glass bottles – this protects the oils from sunlight, which causes them to deteriorate. The shelf life of most oils is up to one year from the day you open a new bottle; citrus oils, like orange, lemon or mandarin, only last six months. Keep your oils in a cool, dark, dry place with the lids on firmly; make sure they are well out of reach of children.

Six key starter essential oils

Lavender *Lavandula angustifolia*

Lavender helps relieve muscular pain and eases headaches, poor sleep and mental stress. Try 2 drops neat Lavender on your pillow for insomnia; 2 drops neat Lavender rubbed into your forehead for a headache; 4 drops Lavender and 4 drops Rosemary in 20 ml/4 teaspoons grapeseed carrier oil massaged into aching muscles.

Rosewood *Aniba rosaeodora*

Rosewood helps dry or mature skin and eases stress and anxiety. Try 4 drops Rosewood and 4 drops Frankincense in 20 ml/4 teaspoons sweet almond carrier oil to soothe dry skin and as a massage oil to help stress.

ROSEWOOD

Frankincense *Boswellia carterii*

Frankincense helps acne, cuts and damaged skin, and soothes mature skin. Use 4 drops Frankincense and 4 drops Tea Tree in 20 ml/4 teaspoons jojoba carrier oil to help damaged skin; try 4 drops Frankincense and 4 drops Rosewood in 20 ml/4 teaspoons sweet almond carrier oil to moisturize mature skin.

Tea Tree *Melaleuca alternifolia*

Tea Tree clears acne, insect bites and skin infections, and helps fight colds and flu. Try 4 drops Tea Tree and 4 drops Frankincense in 20 ml/4 teaspoons jojoba carrier oil on infected skin. 4 drops Tea Tree and 4 drops Lemon in 20 ml/4 teaspoons grapeseed carrier oil helps colds and flu; rub 5 ml/1 teaspoonful of the blend on the chest twice daily.

LAVENDER   FRANKINCENSE

Rosemary *Rosmarinus officinalis*

Rosemary eases muscular spasms and pains, clears
sinuses, and wakes up and stimulates the mind. (Safety
note: Rosemary must not be used by people with
epilepsy.) Use 4 drops Rosemary and 4 drops Lavender
in 20 ml/4 teaspoons grapeseed carrier oil for muscle
spasm. Inhale 3 drops Rosemary on a tissue to help
concentration.

Lemon *Citrus limonum*

Lemon eases sinusitis and blocked noses, relieves stress
and eases depression. Inhale 2 drops Lemon and 2 drops
Rosemary on a tissue for a blocked nose. 4 drops Lemon
and 4 drops Rosewood in 20 ml/4 teaspoons sweet
almond carrier oil is a soothing antidepressant
massage blend.

*Blending essential oils in a vegetable carrier oil makes
them safe to use on the skin.*

How to make a massage blend

This is very simple and takes just a few minutes! Use a
small, clean, dark-glass bottle. Measure your carrier oil
first – a good-quality vegetable oil like sweet almond,
grapeseed or jojoba (good suppliers sell carrier oils as
well as essential oils). Add drops of your chosen
essential oils; put the lid on, shake the
mixture, and it is ready to use. A blend lasts
up to 4 weeks if kept cool.

LEMON LEAF
AND PEEL

*Essential oils are found
in every part of plants
and trees – in the
flowers, leaves, wood,
roots, seeds and fruits.
They are truly the
aromas of nature.*

ROSEMARY

ALMONDS

smell oils for bathtime bliss

One of the best ways to use aromatherapy simply to help you with relaxation and de-stressing is by taking an essential oil bath. Showers serve their purpose, but a bath is definitely a treatment; taking time out to soak in a hot tub can totally change how you feel about yourself and the world around you. To add to the starter kit on the previous pages here are six more lovely essential oils, all from gorgeous far-flung locations, ready to fill your bathroom with exotic aromas.

Bath blends to try

For morning

These blends will wake you up, energize you and improve your mood.

Green Goddess: 3 drops Rosemary, 3 drops Petitgrain

Bright and Alight: 4 drops Frankincense, 2 drops Lemon

Beat the Blues: 3 drops Sweet Orange, 3 drops Mandarin

For evening

These blends are relaxing and nurturing to body and senses – perfect for pampering.

Cleopatra's Garden: 3 drops Mandarin, 3 drops Sandalwood

Tropical Rain: 2 drops Ylang Ylang, 4 drops Rosewood

Orange Surprise: 3 drops Sweet Orange, 3 drops Petitgrain

Twilight Magic: 3 drops Lavender, 3 drops Frankincense

Sweet Dreams: 3 drops Geranium, 3 drops Lavender

essential oils for the bath

oil	from	aroma and effect
Sweet Orange *Citrus sinensis*	Brazil	sweet, soft, relaxing
Sandalwood *Santalum album*	India	woody, spicy, warming
Geranium *Pelargonium graveolens*	Pacific	rosy-sweet, harmonizing, soothing
Petitgrain *Citrus aurantium*	South America	fresh, uplifting
Ylang Ylang *Cananga odorata*	Madagascar	exotic, floral, sensual
Mandarin *Citrus reticulata*	Italy	fresh, sweet, uplifting

GERANIUM

MANDARIN

Aromatherapy bath

10-MINUTE EXERCISE An aromatherapy bath needs some preparation – but it need not take you long. Run your bath to a comfortable temperature, perhaps light a candle on the side, put on a little relaxing music. Choose your combination of essential oils and add them either to 20 ml/4 teaspoons unfragranced bath foam or 20 ml/4 teaspoons full-cream milk – for a touch of Cleopatra, making a milk bath. Both methods soothe the skin and help to disperse the essential oils into the water. Pour in your mixture, swirl it around evenly, and then – get in. Allow yourself a minimum of 10 minutes to soak … oh, go on, have 10 minutes more!

As an extra treat, you can use any of the bath formulae to make a little massage oil as well; so, for example, after a Sweet Dreams bath, add the same essential oil formula to 15 ml/3 teaspoons jojoba carrier oil, and massage your skin with the fragrance you enjoyed in the water. This is a particularly lovely way of helping yourself to relax and de-stress at the end of a long day. You may like to choose one of the ten-minute massage routines in the Touch section of the book.

Let yourself really relax and float away from everyday cares …

smell scenting your environment

Aromatherapy is an excellent way of harnessing the power of the sense of smell to improve your environment. The idea of scenting space is not new; for centuries, aromas have been used to create a particular atmosphere in sacred places like temples and churches. In modern times, aromas are being used in hospitals, schools, hotels and even shops to improve public environments.

By using simple techniques and aromas you enjoy, you can help yourself to cope with the demands of a busy life. Many essential oils have antibacterial properties that help keep the air around you clear and bug-free if other people are suffering from colds and 'flu. Your favourite aromas can be used to improve your mood and help you to concentrate.

The best tool for fragrancing space is a vaporizer, which diffuses the aroma of essential oils into the air over a period of time. There are many electrical models available, which are very safe to use and can be left on for several hours. Ceramic or metal burners, where the oil is warmed from beneath by a small candle, should not be left unattended. Ceramic or metal rings that sit on a light bulb are also available; add your oils carefully and remember to leave the ring to cool down completely before removing it from the bulb.

Add a few drops of essential oil to a ceramic lightbulb ring – the aroma will be released as the ring warms up.

10-minute tip

Inhaling any of these aromas for 10 minutes will make a real difference to your day, clearing your mind and improving your sense of well-being.

special blends for scented spaces

Added to your vaporizer, these blends will fragrance for about an hour.

Home

Place your vaporizer in a corner of the room where you want to enjoy the aromatic effect.

Eating area

3 drops Mandarin and 3 drops Rosemary make a mouth-watering aroma to get the taste buds going.

Kitchen

4 drops Lemon and 2 drops Tea Tree help to clear cooking smells.

Bathroom

3 drops Lavender and 3 drops Sweet Orange make a relaxing aroma.

Bedroom

3 drops Sandalwood and 3 drops Rosewood make a soothing bedtime aroma.

Workplace

An electrical vaporizer can be plugged in next to your computer or on the side in a meeting room.

Desk area

4 drops Lemon and 2 drops Tea Tree will freshen and deodorize your working environment.

Meeting space

3 drops Rosemary and 3 drops Petitgrain make a refreshing blend, promoting mental clarity and creating a stress-free atmosphere.

Car

It is possible to buy vaporizers specially designed for use in the car. You simply put your oils into the unit and then plug it into the cigarette lighter, where the oils are warmed and circulated. Alternatively, you can sprinkle your chosen oils on a tissue and place it on the dashboard.

Vaporizer

3 drops Rosemary and 3 drops Lemon help to keep you awake and alert while driving.

Tissue

Simply put 3 drops Mandarin and 3 drops Tea Tree on the tissue then leave on the dashboard as you drive for a relaxing, fresh aroma.

Enjoy an environment full of the delectable natural aromas of essential oils.

smell time cycles and rhythms

Your sense of smell can help you to link more closely into the rhythms of your day, such as when you wake up in the morning or when you start to wind down later. A great deal of emotional and mental stress arises because of an inability to adapt to the body's need to change tempo at different times – insomnia, for instance, can occur because of an inability to 'switch off' from the demands of the day. Because the sense of smell is so allied to the brain centres responsible for the body's internal chemical balance, it helps to shift mood and change perspectives very quickly.

Essential oils can be used to assist this process very effectively; positive responses to smells like Lavender or Rosewood can be extremely effective at relaxing you into sleep. Children also respond very well to aromas in their environment; fruity aromas like Sweet Orange are comfortingly familiar.

Aroma break

10-MINUTE EXERCISE You can match your essential oils to your moods and the times of the day – start the day with uplifting aromas, use oils that promote harmony at midday, then unwind with floral scents.

Morning

These are oils with aromas that will stimulate and freshen the mind.

Rosemary: Green, bracing, pungent

Tea Tree: Fresh, medicinal

Lemon: Zesty, clean, bright

Frankincense: Uplifting, resiny, sharp

Midday

These are oils with aromas that will harmonize and balance you.

Mandarin: Bitter-sweet, citrusy

Geranium: Rosy-sweet, soft

Sandalwood: Woody, spicy, calming

Petitgrain: Fresh, green, citrusy

Evening

These are oils with aromas that will help you to relax.

Lavender: Floral, soft, fresh

Rosewood: Sweet, woody, soothing

Ylang Ylang: Floral, jasmine-like, sensual

Sweet Orange: Sweet, soft, citrusy

Choose your oils according to aromas you particularly like and feel positive about. If you notice particular stress patterns, such as difficulty waking in the morning, sleeping in the evening, or a lack of vitality in the middle of the day, you can inhale oils from a vaporizer or on a tissue

Children love the sweet, citrusy and soft aroma of Sweet Orange; it can help them sleep.

to help rebalance your mood. Use 4 drops of just one oil, or 3 drops each of a combination of two; take time out, and inhale the aroma for 10 minutes.

Coping with jet lag

If you travel long distance on an aircraft and have trouble adjusting to time-zone changes, use the aromas to help you; the morning oils will help you stay awake and the evening ones will help you relax at times that do not immediately coincide with your 'internal clock'

Use smells to help you cope with the effects of jet lag when you are away from home.

smell aromatic skin and hair treats

Here are some great ideas for skin and hair; these are very quickly prepared and work well if applied for 5 to 10 minutes as a treatment. The ingredients are easy to assemble and are totally natural, with no harsh additives or chemicals to irritate your skin. In addition, the essential oil combinations bring marvellous aromas and wonderful skin-rejuvenating properties into the recipes to enhance your complexion and uplift your spirits. The blends suit dry, combination and mature skins; if you have sensitive or allergy-prone skin, use only half the stated number of drops of oils.

Geranium and Petitgrain oatmeal facial scrub

This paste tones the skin by removing dead skin cells, as well as soothing and softening the surface area. In a small bowl put 30 g/2 tablespoons fine oatmeal, 15 ml/1 tablespoon full-cream milk, 2 drops Geranium and 2 drops Petitgrain. Stir to a paste and apply to the face with small circular movements, massaging carefully for 5 minutes, avoiding the eye area. Wipe off with moist cotton-wool pads, rinse the skin with warm water and pat dry.

Sweet Orange and Rosewood yogurt mask

Natural yogurt is another wonderful natural ingredient that soothes the skin and nourishes the upper cell layers; here jojoba enriches the mixture. In a small bowl put 45 ml/3 tablespoons organic natural yogurt, 5 ml/1 teaspoon jojoba oil, 2 drops Sweet Orange and 2 drops Rosewood. Stir together, apply to the face avoiding the eye area, and leave on for 10 minutes. Wipe off with moist cotton-wool pads, rinse the skin with warm water and pat dry.

Natural ingredients like oatmeal have a softening and extremely soothing effect on the skin.

Lavender and Frankincense
hot oil hair treatment

Aromatic hot oil is a nourishing treat for your hair and scalp. Pour half a litre/20 fl oz of boiling water into a heatproof glass dish. Stand a smaller heatproof bowl in the dish; put in 45 ml/3 tablespoons jojoba carrier oil and add 5 drops Lavender and 4 drops Frankincense. Wait for 3 minutes to heat up the blend, then apply the blend to dry hair and scalp, massaging in well. Wrap a large piece of clingfilm around your head over your hair, followed by a warm towel, and leave for 10 minutes. Remove the towel and film, apply 10 ml/2 teaspoons shampoo directly to your oily hair and rub well, then shower the mixture off. Your hair will gleam and your scalp will tingle.

Sandalwood and
Ylang Ylang super massage oil

This combination of essential and carrier oils is superb for massage, especially for dry skin. In a small dish put 20 ml/4 teaspoons sweet almond carrier oil, add 10 ml/2 teaspoons jojoba and stir together. Add 8 drops Sandalwood and 3 drops Ylang Ylang. Stir again and the blend is ready for application to the skin. Choose one of the ten-minute massage routines on pages 74–79 to apply it ...

It is very easy to adapt your daily skin-care routine to include the use of essential oils and other good-quality natural ingredients.

Touch

Our skin is the point where our world actually comes into contact

with us. It's as if we walk about in a perfectly shaped cloak filled with

super-sensitive nerve endings, so that we can register what we are feeling

in the brain from any part of the body. Think about it now – what can you

feel through your feet, your fingertips, your back? The external

environment feeds you with information via the sense of touch – is it cold,

warm, comfortable, supportive? Certain parts of our skin, like the palms

of our hands, are supersensitive, able to detect the most delicate

sensations. These areas are responsible for our most vivid experiences

of touch, which is the root of all communication.

Touch the essence of care

Touch is at the heart of our daily experience, from the moment we wake to the moment we sleep. Getting dressed, caring for our families, preparing food, eating, working, travelling – everything we do involves coming into direct contact with places and people through the sense of touch. Sometimes that contact is pleasurable, comfortable or intriguing; sometimes it is unpleasant, even painful. When we are in physical discomfort, our nerve receptors send that message through to the brain incredibly quickly. Touch is incredibly sensitive, and influences our direct experience of life.

Babies thrive if they are touched with love and care. It improves their ability to communicate.

If touch is lacking, this can actually cause psychological and physical damage. A study in the USA in the early 20th century involved observing nurses at work in an orphanage in New York; it was noticeable that some babies were picked up and held more than others because of the way they engaged the nurse's attention. These infants put on weight and were much less prone to illness than infants who were not picked up as often. Animal behaviour studies have also shown that if baby animals are deprived of the touch of the mother, even if the sight and smell and sound of her are all available, then weight loss and withdrawn behaviour result. Touch is a life-enhancing requirement in infants, and we still need it very much as adults. Sensory deprivation can bring about disorientation and feelings of isolation.

Touch is a sense that is open to misinterpretation and misuse; if misdirected, it can cause communication to break down between people. It is very important to learn to touch with respect, care and attention. As human beings we are all sensitive, all carrying our own unique feelings and past experiences. Every person

Touch is also a key way of communicating care and security to the brain, which allows a change in our internal biochemical balance to relieve stress and anxiety. Appropriate caring touch is one of the most valuable ways of relaxing and supporting body and mind.

Learning to touch creatures with care helps to build respect for the natural world.

When we touch each other, we need to do so with careful attention and focus.

you meet is a rare and beautiful being. How you approach that being, how you touch them, makes all the difference to that person's life – the difference between a nurturing or a damaging experience. If you are dealing with a rare and delicate plant, for example, it does not make sense to tear the foliage and yank off the flowers. If you touch the plant with respect, feel the delicate beauty of the leaves and the soft petals, then you and the plant will benefit. How we touch each other and the world around us is profoundly important in building a positive relationship with our environment.

Touch switching on the sense

Like many of our senses, touch can become 'switched off' through the stresses of everyday life. We become less attuned to the effects it has because our minds are constantly elsewhere. Then when we try to be aware of it, we may feel somehow that our responses are slow or even lacking. Often, our modern work environments do not encourage touch, or stimulate it creatively; plastic, paper and metal may be all we actually meet during a day. Our hands may become unaccustomed to really feeling.

Here are three ten-minute exercises designed to stimulate your sense of touch through your feet and hands. You will find them relaxing to do in themselves; they slow down your mind and bring a different perspective to your thoughts.

Buddhist walking meditation

10-MINUTE EXERCISE This is ideal for outside on a warm summer day, but you can do it indoors. You need to be bare-footed for this exercise. Simply, you are going to walk slowly around your space – the inside of your home or garden. All the time, you remain silent, you breathe regularly, and you take your awareness into your feet. Feel all the different temperatures and textures under your feet. Cold, warm – these are easy enough. What is the difference between carpet, wood, lino, grass or stone underneath your feet? Notice the sensations and how you feel, and after 10 minutes sit down and relax, thinking about what you experienced.

Learning to focus your attention on touch can be a fascinating process.

Your feet are incredibly sensitive to any subtle changes in temperature and texture. Going bare-foot with awareness of the earth beneath you feels wonderful!

Blindfold touch game

10-MINUTE EXERCISE Try this old-fashioned party game with friends … simply take it in turns to be blindfolded for 10 minutes, during which time you are given different objects to hold and touch to see if you can guess what they are. It's surprising how we rely on sight for identification. This game can be a lot of fun, but be kind to each other and don't use sharp objects! Vegetables, fruit, bowls of things like dry rice or raisins are good to try. It may surprise you how inaccurate you are, which shows you how touch is used mostly in conjunction with other senses to give you information. People who rely on touch, such as those with sight problems, find that it can become incredibly fine-tuned and accurate.

Hand focus

10-MINUTE EXERCISE Explore your space for 10 minutes – either your home or your garden. Touch things with your fingers and hands, and use your focus to really feel the difference between things that are living, like plants or pets, and things that are inert, like stone, glass, metal or ceramic. How does the feel of something alive differ from something that is not? What kinds of textures feel good, what kind do not? Sit down after 10 minutes and consider what you experienced.

Your hands can sense many variations in the texture, shape and feeling of objects.

Touch simple face massage

Massage is a very special form of touch. It involves using particular movements in sequence, working over the skin surface. This really stimulates the skin's touch receptors, as well as warming the area being treated; fresh blood supply is brought to the lower skin layers, giving a flushed appearance, and the sense of touch relays pleasurable sensations to the brain. Deep relaxation and stress relief are the result.

Face massage is very easy to administer yourself in front of the mirror. To work easily on delicate facial skin, as well as to nourish and feed it, it is good to use a rich carrier oil like jojoba. This is a liquid plant wax that gives a silky but non-greasy feel to the skin. Here are some face blends to make up with combinations of essential oils; choose a blend to suit your skin type.

Choose essential oil blends to suit your own skin type. The oils help to nourish and rejuvenate the skin.

Base: 20 ml/4 teaspoons jojoba (enough for 3 to 4 applications)

Blends

Dry/mature skin: 3 drops Sandalwood, 2 drops Frankincense

Combination/oily skin: 3 drops Geranium, 2 drops Lemon

Sensitive skin: 1 drop Rosewood, 1 drop Lavender

First, cleanse and exfoliate the skin using the Geranium and Petitgrain oatmeal facial scrub on page 66. Pat dry, then you are ready to apply the blend.

Facial self-massage sequence

10-MINUTE EXERCISE **1** Take 5 ml/1 teaspoon of your chosen blend into your hand and work it into your fingers a little bit, then apply it quickly over the face, starting at the forehead, working around the eye area, then over the cheeks, nose and chin, to the neck.

2 Place your hands so the ends of your fingertips meet together in the middle of your forehead. Using tiny little circular movements with all fingers, work from the middle of the forehead out to the sides, to your temples. Bring the fingers back to the middle and repeat twice more.

3 Using the first and middle fingers on each hand, start between the eyebrows and gently work your way outwards around your bony eye sockets, pressing down briefly then moving on. Make circles all around your eye areas. Then make tiny circular movements down each side of your nose, from between the eyebrows down to the tip. Repeat this sequence.

4 Using all your fingertips, make tiny circular movements down your cheeks, from the cheekbones to the chin. Make a circle of tiny pressures all around your lips; then use your first finger and thumb on both hands, meeting in the middle of your chin, to massage along your jaw out to the side. Repeat this sequence.

5 Using the palms of both hands, make gentle sweeping movements upwards under your chin. Continue these strokes up your cheeks, over your nose and forehead to your hairline. Rest your hands on your forehead to finish.

Touch hand-care massage routine

This is a routine you can either do for yourself or receive from a friend. The hands work incredibly hard each day, performing thousands of repetitive movements. They grasp, stretch, grip and are also capable of picking up minute objects. Even the most complex robots cannot simulate the simple grace of the human hand as it moves, thanks to bones, muscles and tendons all working together in sequence. If you have any hand injuries or any arthritis or joint problems, hand massage must be very gentle. The warming effects will help to improve mobility.

It is good to use an aromatherapy blend for hand massage to nourish dry, damaged skin, as well as improve circulation. Sweet almond carrier oil has been used in hand care for centuries to soften and smooth the skin. If you have eczema or any skin irritation, then use half the number of stated drops of essential oils in the same amount of carrier oil.

Super hand-care blend

To 20 ml/4 teaspoons sweet almond oil, add 4 drops Frankincense, 2 drops Lavender, 2 drops Rosewood (enough for 2 to 3 applications)

LAVENDER

ALMONDS

Hand self-massage sequence

10-MINUTE EXERCISE Spend 5 minutes on each hand. Work on the right hand first.

1 Stroke 5 ml/1 teaspoon of the blend onto the upper surface of the hand, from the fingertips up towards the wrist, 3 times, then turn the hand over and stroke again, from the fingertips, over the palm and up to the wrist, 3 times.

2 Keeping the palm upwards, press your thumb into the centre and make several slow circles around the area, feeling the bones stretch out as you do so. This is great for warming the whole hand.

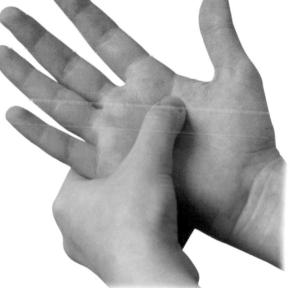

3 Massage each finger and the thumb in turn, making small circles with your thumb and fingers from the tip downwards. This improves the circulation. Give each finger and thumb a gentle stretch when you have finished.

4 Return to the upper surface of the hand; stroke firmly from the fingertips to the wrist several times, then finish with feather-light strokes over the whole area.

Repeat the whole sequence on the left hand.

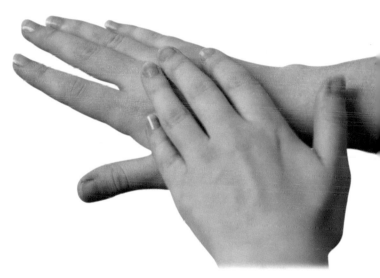

Once you have learned this hand massage sequence, you will find it is something you can use anywhere to ease out aches in the hands and improve circulation. This is also a very useful technique to know if, for example, you are visiting someone who is unwell or in hospital – it is very quick to give, and pleasant and reassuring to receive.

Touch fabulous foot-soothing treat

Feet are often ignored or even disliked, which is a pity because they are particularly wonderful things. Bones are cushioned by muscles and stretched by tendons to enable us to put one foot in front of the other and walk. Considering the uncomfortable shoes we often force our poor feet into, they manage very well. They bear our weight and carry us through our lives with very few thanks from us. In Roman times, it was customary to bathe and massage the feet of important guests when they arrived in your home; it was a mark of care and respect. Imagine doing that for your friends!

You will be amazed at how rejuvenating and energizing a foot massage can be. Even if you are tired when you begin, the combination of foot massage and aromatherapy oils will bring a sense of zest. It's easy to do and a great way to prepare for a night on the town!

Ten-minute soak

If you have time, a great way to prepare the feet for massage is to put 3 litres/6 pints of warm water into a large bowl with 4 drops Rosemary essential oil and soak your feet for 10 minutes. This is a great way to relax your feet and legs if you have to stand for long periods during the day.

Foot massage balm

Use 20 ml/4 teaspoons grapeseed oil carrier; this is not too greasy and leaves the feet soft and smooth. Add 6 drops Rosemary, 4 drops Lemon essential oils

Your feet will really appreciate a massage with refreshing essential oils blended in a nourishing carrier oil.

5 Massage each toe individually from the tip downwards, giving each one a little stretch to follow.

6 Finally, use both hands together to stroke the upper and lower surfaces of the foot at the same time, from the tip of the toes towards the ankle and back, several times. This really warms the circulation.

Repeat the whole sequence on the left foot.

Foot massage is very calming and soothing to give and receive, and has extra benefits – by massaging over the surface of the feet you are giving gentle stimulation to reflex points used in reflexology, which benefits the whole body.

Foot self-massage sequence

10-MINUTE EXERCISE Spend 5 minutes on each foot. Work on the right foot first.

1 Take 5 ml/1 teaspoon of the balm and apply it quickly all over the surfaces of the foot.

2 Using the heel of your left hand – the soft pad at the base of the palm – rub up and down under the arch of your foot several times.

3 Use the same part of the hand to make circles over the heel and under the ball of the foot. These movements feel good – they stretch all the little bones.

4 With one hand on each side, use both your hands to rub the upper surface of the foot.

Touch neck and shoulder relief

The neck and shoulders are classic stress points. Sitting crouched over work or in a stiff position in the car while driving, holding the phone under your ear, carrying heavy bags on one side of the body – these are all things that, over time, cause the muscles in the neck and shoulders to become hard and painful – in spasm. If nothing is done, in addition to pain there may be knock-on effects like migraines, which can affect you seriously. If you are experiencing persistent pain or problems in this area, it is wise to consult a doctor or a physiotherapist.

This simple neck and shoulder routine can be done fully clothed, so it works well anywhere you happen to be. Find a chair with a stable back; sit comfortably and lean on the back for support. The person giving the massage then stands behind you.

2

Neck and shoulder massage allows the area to be warmed, stretched and gently worked. It works best if you receive it from someone else because you cannot easily reach the key areas yourself. If you are giving the massage, make sure your friend is comfortable with what you are doing – keep checking as you work. Keep your movements smooth and slow; this is much more deeply relaxing.

Neck and shoulder massage sequence

10-MINUTE EXERCISE

1 First, place one hand on the top of each of your friend's shoulders, and lean down gently to give a stretch to the area. You will feel warmth under your hands, and this firm, gentle touch is very calming to receive in itself. Wait at least 30 seconds.

2 Still with the hands in the same position, start to squeeze the muscles in the top of the shoulder gently. They may feel very hard, so work slowly; the movement is called 'kneading', and it is a bit like making bread! Check with your friend that the pressure feels comfortable. Do this for 3 minutes.

3 Still with one hand on each side, apply a row of pressures with your thumbs, across the top of the shoulders, out to the sides, down around the shoulder blades, and back up on either side of the spine. The shoulder blades are large, triangular-shaped bones and are easy to feel. Repeat this sequence for 3 minutes.

4 Ask your friend to sit up straight and put your right hand over their forehead to support them against you. With your left hand, gently massage up and down on either side of the bones in the neck, using tiny circular movements with your thumb and fingers, for 2 minutes. Gently release the head.

4

Touch relaxing back massage

Lying somewhere warm and comfortable, with all the tension and stress being massaged out of your back, preferably using a lovely fragrant body oil, is one of the most beautifully relaxing experiences. It is wonderful to give and receive, and creates a sense of trust and communication between two people. Massage applied directly on the skin concentrates the mind on pure sensation, and warm touch soothes aches and pains as well as easing emotional tension.

The room needs to be warm, and the person being massaged should lie on a mat or futon cushion covered with fluffy towels, propped up with pillows so they are totally comfortable. The massage is given kneeling beside the person; it is better to work on the floor, which is firm, rather than on a bed where the springs tend to give under your weight. You need to kneel by your friend's hips, on whichever side feels most comfortable to you.

Three back-massage blends

Base: 4 teaspoons/20ml sweet almond carrier oil (enough for a single application)

Relaxing: 3 drops Lavender, 3 drops Rosewood, 4 drops Mandarin

Invigorating: 4 drops Rosemary, 3 drops Lemon, 3 drops Petitgrain

Sensual: 4 drops Sweet Orange, 2 drops Ylang Ylang, 4 drops Sandalwood

MANDARIN

ROSEMARY

82

Back massage sequence

10-MINUTE EXERCISE **1** First, pour at least 1 teaspoon/5ml of the chosen blend into the palm of your hand, then smooth it quickly over the whole surface area of the back. If the skin is very dry, you may need to use all of it. The aim is to have the surface of the skin feeling supple, not drenched with blend, or your hands will slip too much.

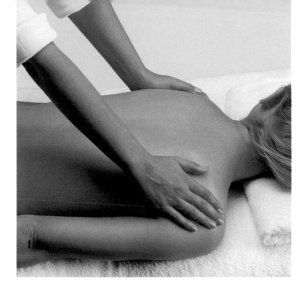

2 Place both hands at the base of the back on either side of the spine. Slowly stroke all the way up to the shoulders, out to the sides and down the outside of the torso to the starting point. Repeat at least 6 times— more if your friend's skin is cold.

3 Next, starting back at the base of the spine, place your hands side by side and fan out from the center to the side of the torso, 3 times over the lower back, 3 times over the mid back, and 3 times over the upper back. Repeat this sequence once.

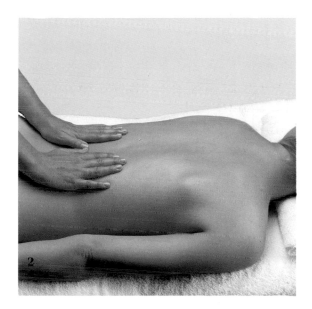

4 Starting at the base of the spine, thumbs on either side of the spinal bones, make 2 lines of pressures up toward the shoulders, moving your thumbs up about 1 inch/2 cm each time. Check with your friend that the pressure is comfortable. Repeat this sequence once.

5 Finally, repeat the stroke in Step 2, several times, slowing down as you finish.

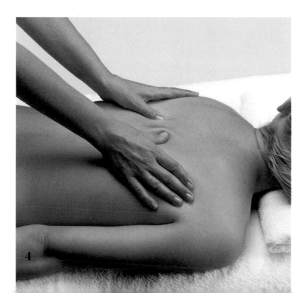

Touch tranquil tummy massage

The abdomen is an area where many of us store our stress and tension. The solar plexus, the major nerve centre right up under the rib cage, is where we register extreme anxiety as pain, tightness or 'butterflies in the stomach'. This is equally true for both children and adults. The abdomen is also a very personal area, and because it is so sensitive we may not feel comfortable having it touched by another person. However, self-massage of the abdomen is easy to administer.

Abdomen massage not only relieves tightness associated with stress, it also helps discomfort caused by problems such as indigestion or period pain, which may also have a link to emotional stress.

It is really useful to apply essential oils in a blend here; many oils soothe pain and relieve cramps as well as easing emotional tension. If you want to use blends and massage on children aged 2 to 10 years, use half the stated number of drops in the same amount of carrier oil. Older children can be treated with the full amount of essential oil. Baby blends are on page 86.

Tummy massage blends

Peppermint (*Mentha piperita*) essential oil is a classic for tummy pain and problems; it relieves pain and spasm and soothes the whole area. Here are two blends to choose from featuring this special oil.

Base: 20ml/4 teaspoons sweet almond carrier oil (enough for 2 to 3 applications)
Soothing, calming, pain-relieving: 6 drops Lavender, 2 drops Peppermint, 2 drops Sandalwood
Soft and soothing, good for period pains: 6 drops Sweet Orange, 2 drops Geranium, 2 drops Peppermint

PEPPERMINT

Tummy self-massage sequence

10-MINUTE EXERCISE Sit comfortably somewhere warm and quiet.

1 Take 5 ml/1 teaspoon of your chosen blend into your right hand and smooth it all over your abdominal area, covering all the skin surface.

2 Starting at your right hip, using your right hand, stroke up under your rib cage, down your left side and across your lower abdomen, making a complete circle. Repeat this 5 times. Keep the movement slow and firm.

3 Using both hands, starting at your sides, criss-cross the hands over the top of your abdomen, slowly, 5 times.

4 Repeat the circling movement from Step 2, using both hands together, starting at the right hip and moving up and around 5 times. The abdomen should feel warm and soothed.

5 Now cover the abdomen with a towel and place a hot-water bottle on top while you sit and relax. The heat helps the oils to penetrate and also relieves pain and tension.

This sequence can be given to another person; the main thing to remember if you are massaging someone else's tummy is that your touch needs to be gentle and respectful; concentrate on the warmth of your hands to give them maximum comfort.

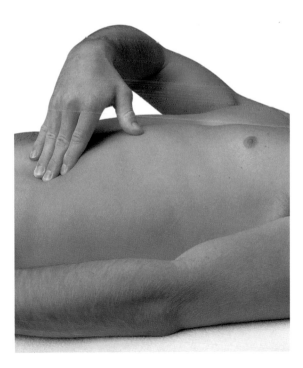

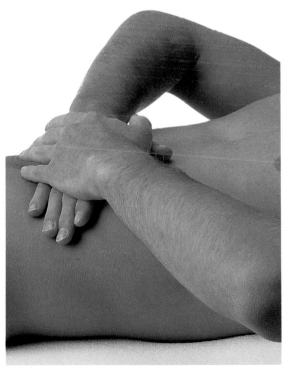

Touch baby and infant massage

In many cultures, it is a totally natural thing to massage babies; in Tahiti, a special oil called monoi, made of gardenia flowers infused in coconut oil, is applied daily to baby skin as a nourishing moisturizer. Massage encourages good health, good emotional balance and good skin tone, and keeps digestion regular, as well as building a very important tactile bond between parent and child. Babies respond very well to touch, and ten minutes is a very suitable massage routine for them.

After the bath is a particularly good time to work, just before bedtime.

You need to work in a very warm room, and have your baby lying comfortably on warm towels. Some gentle music and soft light help to create a warm and soothing atmosphere. You can use the massage as a kind of game, an opportunity to laugh and smile and make lovely positive contact with your baby.

Baby blends

Base: 20 ml/4 teaspoons sweet almond carrier oil (enough for 3 to 4 applications). Notice the very tiny amount of essential oil used here – this is because of the delicate state of a baby's skin.

To help sleep: 1 drop Lavender
To soothe dry skin: 1 drop Rosewood
To help eczema: 1 drop Roman Camomile
To balance digestion: 1 drop Sweet Orange

Make baby massage a special time to enjoy lovely caring contact between you and your baby.

Baby massage sequence

10-MINUTE EXERCISE **1** Make sure your hands are warm when you start. Try lying the baby on its back to begin with; engage his or her attention with sounds and smiles. Put 5 ml/1 teaspoon of your chosen blend into your hand, then very gently apply to the tummy in small, circular motions.

2 Spread your movements up the chest and over the shoulders, making little circles with your fingers as you go, then down the arms and to the hands, onto the legs and down to the feet. Really pause on the hands and feet and enjoy massaging the tiny palms, soles, fingers and toes.

3 Gently turn the baby over, and apply 2.5 ml/half a teaspoon of the blend onto the back, smoothing it over the skin from the shoulders to the buttocks, always keeping your movements circular and flowing.

4 Take the circular movements down the backs of the legs to the feet, then stroke down the whole body to finish. Cover the baby to keep lovely and warm.

Elements of this massage routine can be used to calm your baby in stressful moments; the downward stroking on the back is particularly effective, bringing the security of your touch to the very sensitive nerve endings along the spine itself. The important thing about your touch is that it should be sensitive but also confident, with warm hands communicating a sense of safety and peace.

Make sure your movements are tiny and very precise.

Take the little, circular movements down the hands to the feet.

Touch acupressure for stress relief

Acupressure, similar to acupuncture, is another technique that can help deal with stress. It is based on the idea that our physical structure is not just made up of bones, muscles and tendons; there are also energy lines called 'meridians' that follow specific pathways throughout the whole body, passing through all the major organs on the way. Applying pressure to these points releases the flow of energy that has been 'stuck', and rebalances the channel, the organ affected and the whole system.

The body is covered with hundreds of points that link up to form the 'meridians'.

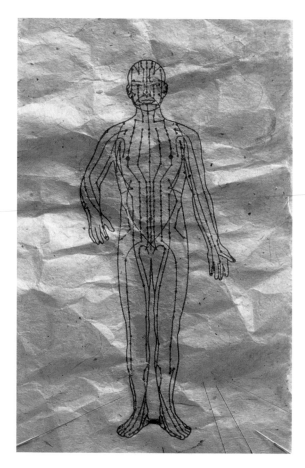

It takes many years to become a practitioner of acupuncture or acupressure; however, there are some simple techniques that you can apply yourself to help rebalance your energies. You should use the soft pads at the end of your thumb or fingers to apply gentle but firm pressure for 5 seconds, then release. Acupressure can be applied while clothed.

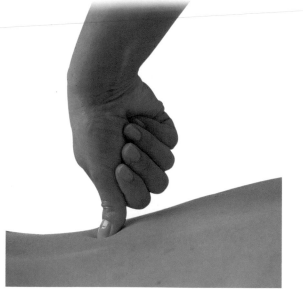

Head and neck acupressure sequence

10-MINUTE EXERCISE This sequence eases mental stress and headaches or heavy feelings in the head, and helps improve concentration, for example if you work on a computer.

1 Working on the crown of your head as if your hair were parted down the middle, starting at the hairline at the top of the forehead, use the first 2 fingers of your right hand to make a line of 6 pressures towards the back of your head. Each pressure should last about 5 seconds. Repeat this sequence once.

2 Using the first 3 fingers on each hand, apply gentle pressure to your temples, next to your eyes. Do 3 pressures of 5 seconds each.

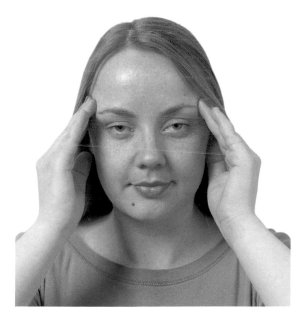

3 Using all 4 fingers and both hands, apply 2 rows of pressure to the back of your neck, on either side of the neck bones. Do 3 pressures of 5 seconds each.

Lower back acupressure sequence

10-MINUTE EXERCISE If you sit all day at a desk, or drive a car for long periods, or do gardening, this is a really easy self-help sequence to use in the evening to ease stress, aches and tiredness. You need to rest your fingers either side of your waist and use your thumbs to apply pressure.

1 Start halfway up your back, thumbs either side of the spine. Make 5 pressures, each for 5 seconds, down towards the base of your spine. Repeat.

2 With your hands at hip level, your thumbs as far in as they will go, make 3 pressures in a row outwards, for 5 seconds. Repeat.

3 With your fingers lower down and your thumbs in the middle of your buttocks, make 4 pressures diagonally up towards the base of your spine. Repeat.

Hearing

Our sense of hearing is acutely tuned to the outside world. What we register as sound are in fact ripples of air molecules being moved in a particular way; these movements are picked up by the receiving dish of our ear and they make the eardrum vibrate. This then influences three tiny bones in the inner ear, called the hammer, the anvil and the stirrup. These move in the fluid of the inner ear, touching microscopic hairs that trigger nerves to send messages to the brain, so we 'hear'. The act of hearing means we translate the movement of air into ripples of inner ear fluid, then finally into electrical impulses, which we interpret as sound.

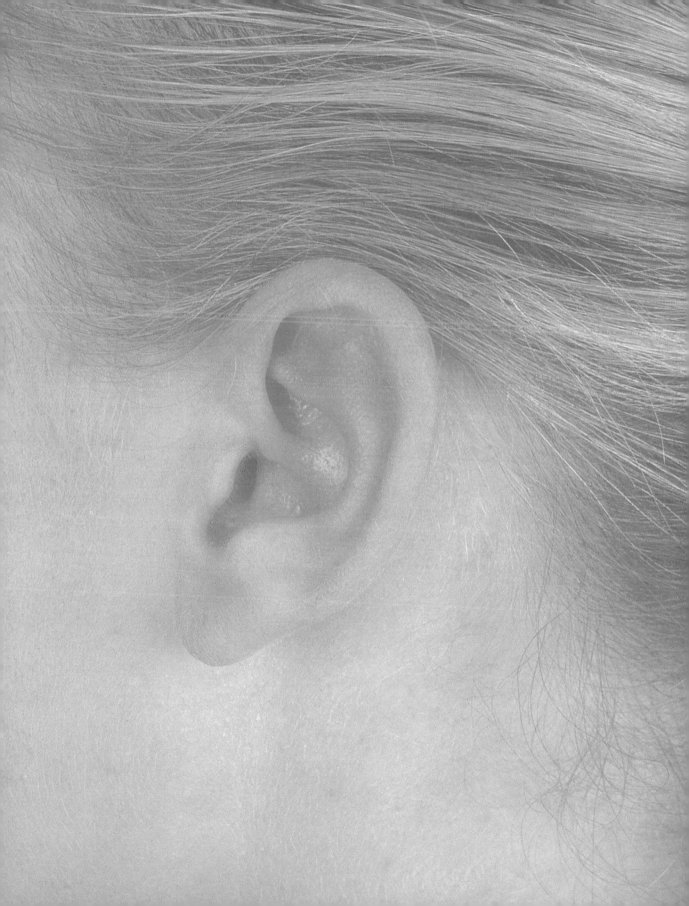

Hearing sound, noise and silence

If you go somewhere truly deep into nature, such as high into mountains or into the depths of a wood, you may be struck by the deep sense of peace that spreads through such places. There are sounds to be heard, but these are very different to the hustle and bustle of the modern world. The sounds of nature are hugely varied – the rustle of a bird in a tree, wind stirring the grass, an insect's wings whirring, a stream running somewhere. In this kind of space you may become more aware of your own inner sounds – your heartbeat, even the sound of your blood pumping through your veins.

In contrast, you may be unaware of how much your space is filled with the sounds of machinery. The mechanical noise of engines has changed the background sound of the modern world. Aircraft, trains, metro systems, industrial processes, sirens, household equipment, DIY drills – all these things surround us with a continuous barrage of noise. These sounds, if they reach particular levels, can cause tension and ill health; local councils find noise complaints at the top of the list of typical neighbour disturbances. Sometimes disputes over noise can create almost unbearable tension between people. Why? Because all sounds are picked up by our sensitive ears, and if someone else is generating unpleasant levels of noise, it can feel like an invasion of personal space.

What is silence? It is actually something we very rarely experience; even when we sleep we are aware of sounds and they still register. In almost any situation, even in the most removed natural environment, there will be sounds. In some buildings, such as cathedrals, silence may be easier to experience; the building is like a great shell that contains the space inside it. If you can be there when there is nothing going on, then perhaps total silence may be found. It is not just an absence of noise; it is a state of inner peace where everything just calms down. Complete silence can be deeply restoring to the whole system.

Even outside in the natural environment, there will be sounds of some kind – the wind rustling through the leaves, for example. However, these natural sounds are very soothing to the mind.

Sensing sounds around you

10-MINUTE EXERCISE Just sit down and relax wherever you happen to be. Now extend your sense of hearing and just explore all the sounds you can pick up around you, from wherever they may be coming. What kinds of sounds can you hear? Can you identify them all?

Try and write them down, and think about how they arise – are they mechanical or are they natural? Notice how you feel about these sounds. Do you block them out normally? How does identifying these sounds make you feel about your environment?

Sound, noise and silence   93

Hearing the nature of sound

If you put your hands on a stereo speaker, you will be able to feel the vibration of the sounds coming out of it. The waves of movement that make up the sounds vibrate at different rates. The human ear can pick up frequencies of between 20 and 20,000 hertz (1 hertz = 1 cycle per second). Male voices register at around 100 cycles per second, females at 150 – a woman's voice sounds 'higher pitched' than a man's. A soprano singing a high C registers at over 1,000 hertz; the higher the hertz frequency, the higher the pitch. A plane flying by registers at around 100 hertz, a much lower frequency.

We are also affected by the intensity of sounds, or how loud or soft they are; this is measured in decibels (dB). Silence is measured at 0 dB, whispered speech at 30 dB, normal conversation at 60 dB, a vacuum cleaner at 75 dB. Shouting goes up to 80dB; sound becomes very uncomfortable to the ear at over 100 dB (a pneumatic drill close by). Rock concerts or raves often register at over 110 dB, the point when hearing can become painful; intense sounds at over 140 dB will totally damage hearing by destroying the tiny hair-like membranes in the inner ear that relay sound to the brain.

Incredibly, science has found ways to show the actual shapes of some sound vibrations. Experiments with wave generators, where sounds have been projected across powders, pastes and liquids, have created incredible patterns like snowflakes, winding ribbons or swirling eddies; sounds are actually capable of rearranging physical particles. Work with plants has shown that plants grow stronger and taller when exposed to particular sound frequencies – the idea of 'talking to your plants' is not so crazy after all. Sound actually affects structure. Beneficial sound at the right

The right sound frequencies can encourage strong, healthy growth in plants.

frequency and intensity will be soothing, nourishing and relaxing; if it is too low, too high or too loud, it can actually be damaging.

The sound of instruments like Tibetan singing bowls can slow our brain waves from the active Beta state and help to bring about the Delta waves of deep relaxation.

Our brains also generate four types of waves which can be measured in hertz.

Alpha waves

8–13 hertz

These are present when you are awake and resting with eyes closed. They disappear during sleep.

Beta waves

14–30 hertz

These appear when you are awake and pursuing normal activity.

Theta waves

4–7 hertz

These occur when you are under emotional stress.

Delta waves

1–5 hertz

These occur during sleep and states of deep relaxation.

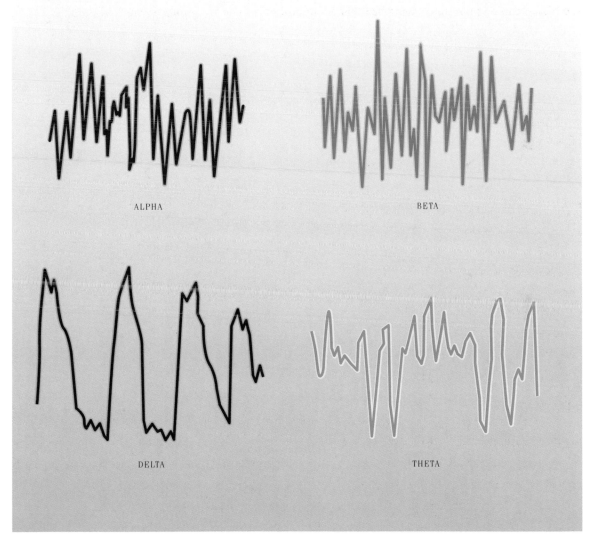

ALPHA

BETA

DELTA

THETA

Hearing silence for healing

Many people find the idea of silence rather daunting. We are so used to the pattern of sounds that accompanies every aspect of our daily lives that the thought of being quiet feels empty. The space that is created when all is quiet takes a little getting used to, which is why ten minutes is an ideal length of time to practise the exercises given here. They are best done first thing in the morning or last thing at night, just before sleep. Either way, you will benefit from the slowing down of thought processes and the simplicity of sitting quietly, resting your mind and calming your heartbeat.

Preparation

The easiest posture to adopt for comfort is to sit on a dining chair with a firm back to support you. If you lie down, you will probably fall asleep, and it is not easy to relax while sitting cross-legged on the floor – this is an eastern meditation posture, which can be tricky to maintain if you are not used to it. Wear loose, comfortable clothes and put a warm shawl around your shoulders; when you sit still you can feel chilly. If you wish, you can light a candle; this helps to create a warm focus in the room.

Silent contemplation 1

10-MINUTE EXERCISE Take 3 smooth, deep breaths, then breathe normally. Relax. Let your hands sit comfortably in your lap. Close your eyes if you wish. Be aware of the quiet all around you like a cloak;

Take time to tune in to the total peace and stillness to be found deep within you.

rest into that sense of space. Now simply take your awareness to your breath, and follow its pattern, in and out, regularly. When your attention drifts, just gently guide it back to the breath. If thoughts come, just let them dissolve. Keep focusing on the rhythm of your breath. After 10 minutes, stretch fingers and toes and slowly let your awareness come back into the room.

Silent contemplation 2

10-MINUTE EXERCISE Take 3 deep breaths, then breathe normally. Relax. Close your eyes if you wish. In your mind's eye, visualize a calm lake. See the translucent beauty of the still water, unruffled, for there is no breeze, no sound, just complete tranquillity. The water may be deep blue, or softly silver, or pink with the glow of a sunset. Let your imagination paint this picture

for you; it may be a place you know, or an image that you create. Either is fine. Rest with this image for 10 minutes, then stretch fingers and toes and let your awareness come back into the room.

Make sure you are sitting comfortably and that you wear warm clothes, so that you can relax.

The stillness of a lake is a beautiful image that helps you to build a sense of inner calm and quiet.

Hearing music for body and soul

Humans are the only species on the planet able to create and make music. Insects, animals and birds make sounds, some of which are elaborate and may even be at frequencies beyond the human ear, but none of these creatures have the ability to conjure up sounds and put them together in complex musical patterns, as people have done for millennia. Prehistoric excavations have yielded primitive instruments like drums and rattles, showing that humankind's relationship with sound-making is very ancient.

Scientific studies have shown that music can evoke feelings of intense joy, shifts in mood and deep emotional responses, stirring the sense of hearing to heights of pleasure. This is felt in the body as tingling sensations, in the mind as a sense of heightened feeling and in the spirit as a kind of timeless rapture. It is no wonder that every age has produced its forms of music, every culture on the planet has its traditional instruments and sounds. In Europe, the simplicity of medieval plainsong chant gave way to the complex interweaving harmonies of the Renaissance called polyphony – the discovery of chords, multiple sounds that resonated with each other and filled the ears with new sensations. Each successive era has produced different combinations of music through a variety of experimentation with sound.

There are so many forms of music to choose from – classical, jazz, folk, traditional, modern, rock, electronic – all of which affect the listener in different ways.

Choosing a special piece of music that gives you pleasure is a treat for your ears.

The intricate notes of the harp are particularly calming and often recall images of water.

However, if you want to listen to music for a particularly relaxing and de-stressing effect, it is very hard to beat classical composers like Johann Sebastian Bach. Bach's music is astonishing in its perfection – the sounds he has created are within a frequency band that is perfect for bringing about a calming and clarifying effect.

Active listening

10-MINUTE EXERCISE Active listening means applying your focus to what you are hearing, rather than letting music just drift over you. You need to sit comfortably, in a relaxed posture, and either use headphones or ensure you can listen undisturbed. Choose one of the following pieces, all of which last approximately 10 minutes, or a piece you enjoy. As the music plays, let your mind focus on what you are hearing. Do you pick out individual themes or notes, or are you listening to the whole of what is being played? Notice how you feel after 10 minutes of the following:

- 'Sanctus' from Mass in B Minor by JS Bach
- Organ Fantasia and Fugue in G Minor by JS Bach
- Canon by Pachelbel
- Kyrie and Gloria from Missa Papae Marcelli by Palestrina
- Adagio – Piano Concert No 2 by Rachmaninov

Hearing using your own voice

Your own voice box produces the sound that is unique to you. Think of all the people you know and the way you can recognize them from the sound of their voices. Multiply that by different languages with all their styles and intonations and sounds, and you realize how we populate the planet with vocal variety. Speaking normally allows you to use the frequencies of your particular language; this is how we communicate. However, yet again, the human species goes further. We can sing.

Now, before we continue – yes, many of us have been told as children that we were tone-deaf and a pain to listen to, and the idea of singing makes us recoil; but often this was allied to pressure around performance. We all have a unique ability to make sounds, and exercising the voice is actually extremely beneficial to our inner health. Remember, sounds and vibrations affect physical structure; different sounds can affect brain wave patterns and so give us a real sense of deep relaxation.

The different sound vibrations of the five vowels work at different energetic levels in the body.

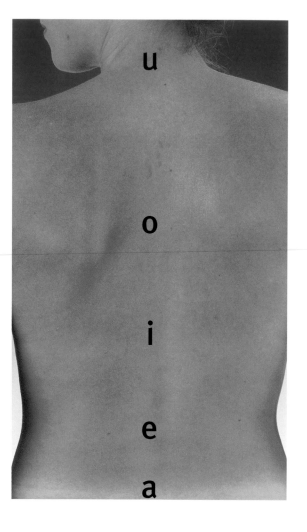

sounds linked to chakras

u	(pronounced 'oo')	throat
o	(to rhyme with 'toe')	heart
i	(to rhyme with 'me')	solar plexus
e	(to rhyme with 'bed')	sacral
a	(to rhyme with 'car')	base or root

Exercising your voice is a way of releasing your personal sound, and the more you do it, the more you may find you want to sing. It is a marvellous group activity, whether you tackle great choral works or simple chants and songs; sharing your voice with others is a wonderful way to feel the beneficial and uplifting power of sound. In Africa, no traditional village ceremony is complete without songs, many of which have deeply sacred meaning and involve the whole community.

Before you begin to chant the vowel sounds, always take in a good deep breath. Make sure the breath fills your diaphragm so that you can feel your ribs expand, and use the air to make the sound.

From the tradition of yoga comes the idea that the main vowel sounds – a, e, i, o, u – are linked to vibratory centres called 'chakras', which run up the spine. The chart shows those relationships.

Sound treatment

10-MINUTE EXERCISE This is very relaxing to do and you do not need to bring the house down; chant at a pitch that is comfortable to your voice and do not strain. Sit comfortably with your hands resting loosely on your lap. As you chant each vowel, starting at 'a', visualize the part of the body that links to it. You are actually giving yourself a 'sound treatment'.

Chant each vowel 3 times: a, e, i, o, u. Notice how the sounds make you feel as you chant them. Then breathe gently and relax.

3 Intuition/SixthSense

Once you have an enhanced understanding of how each individual sense works, you may be wondering – do they combine with each other? Human experience involves a synergy, or a working together of all the senses to give us the huge input of information that makes up our daily life. We can go beyond just simply soaking up sensory impressions; we are capable of taking the input we are given and developing something out of it – we can harness sensory capability to create something new. We can use the senses to help us de-stress and relax and also be more in touch with our environment; but we can also use our creativity to take us into new experiences that are both enriching and fulfilling.

sixth sense sensory synergy

Synergy is what happens when lots of things combine together to create something more powerful than any one of them individually. Synergy is exciting and challenging and is the gateway to creative expression. It is open to everyone, regardless of age or so-called ability; all of us have the tools, the magnificent five senses that we have been given through our evolution. Exploring creativity is working with synergy. It involves the intuition, the 'small voice' inside, which is so often right in what it suggests but usually gets ignored.

Getting in touch with synergy is a wonderful way of appreciating how the senses can work together. Here is an exercise that is presented through a picture, but you can also do it by actually going to such a location, if you can, and allowing the play of your senses to guide you. It is 'play': explore the ideas with a sense of fun and interest, be aware of the resulting effects on you, and the fact that you are unique – your impressions are your very own.

Picture the sea

 You may wish to record this on a tape to help you. Pause at the end of each sentence to let your impressions form in your mind.

Here is a beautiful image of the sea. Sit and let the image fill your vision, relax and breathe comfortably. After a few moments, close your eyes and let the picture come to life in your mind's eye.

The sea is a marvellous location, creating an effect that is both energizing and relaxing.

What kind of sensory impressions come to you as the image fills your mind? Are they visual, linked to the landscape, the colours, the depths of the water? Are they heard, linked to the sound of the waves, the rushing of water over stones on the beach? Are you aware of the smell of the brine, the tang of seaweed? Can you taste salt in your mouth? Are you itching to put your feet in the water and let it rush around your toes? Concentrate on the image of the sea and let the sensations fill you. You may find one sense particularly dominates your awareness; try and let the input of the others come through as well.

Now, instead of being aware of individual sensory impressions, relax, and just let the whole image of 'sea' fill your awareness. You don't have to try; just breathe and let it happen. How does this feel? Sit quietly for a few moments and let this impression flow through you. Then stretch fingers and toes and let yourself come back to the room.

Getting in touch with that 'whole' image can be quite magical – a point where you actually experience a kind of relationship with the special qualities it brings. Try this exercise outside in different locations you particularly love.

sixth sense sensory creativity

If you feel you do not know how to be creative and what that actually means, you can use your senses to guide you into exploring your own world in a new and fun way. This has the effect of bringing qualities of joy, fun and lightness into your experience; you tend to find that daily stresses are dissolved in the excitement of finding out new things. Much of our stress is linked to boredom, to the fact that our lives seem to be full of endless tasks that demand our energy but don't reward us personally. Getting in touch with your own unique creative energy can change all that.

Not being creative is often expressed as 'I can't draw' or 'I can't make things'; unfortunately our attitudes to ourselves have often been shaped long ago in childhood. They may be linked to pressure around performing, or to attitudes that told us 'it's a waste of time' or 'stop doing nothing'. Changing these attitudes is very important. As a human being it is your right to create, to express yourself in ways that reflect who you are. Landmarks such as the Eiffel Tower in Paris, Stonehenge in Wiltshire and Tower Bridge in London were all the result of creativity. We draw so much from these and other special monuments and sites, because when we visit them we still marvel at how on earth they were created. We might not be able to do things on the same scale, but there is creative potential in each and every one of us.

Once you appreciate the individual gifts of each one of the five senses, you can use them to enhance your creative output. As you do this, you may very well find that the other senses are working in tandem; you begin to experience synergy. How do you know? You feel thrilled, you laugh, you lose track of time and you can seem to go on for hours without noticing. Suddenly you

Get in touch with materials such as clay, which you can work with and shape yourself.

have more than enough energy. It's absolutely wonderful. Anyone can do it. Give yourself short bursts of time to try things out, and you may suddenly find yourself 'on a roll', with enthusiasm to keep going for the sheer joy of it.

In the next few pages you will find ideas to get you started in different sensory ways. Choose a sense you

Let yourself expand through your senses and enjoy your potential to the full.

feel really in tune with and start something … remember, a thousand-mile journey starts with one step! There are no mistakes, this is not a performance – it's an opportunity for you to have fun and learn.

sixth sense creative sight

If you are a visual person, you will react powerfully to colour – it may even stop you in your tracks, particular shades just making your mouth water. When did you last pick up a paintbrush? Was it to decorate your living space? How would it be to use colour just for the fun of it? We are not talking about turning you into a Michelangelo here, but you may have undiscovered talents – who knows? Using colour, choosing shades instinctively and merging them together is exciting and fun. Succulent pinks, lush greens, vibrant golds are enticing.

You need some equipment here – the best place to get it is a children's shop where paints and paper in different colours and sizes will be readily available. Get some brightly coloured paints and a large brush that feels comfortable to hold in your hand. Also, get the biggest size of paper you can. We are going for space! You can always pretend you are buying things for a niece or nephew ... but you will know you are buying them for yourself, and that can be a source of fun!

It's good to paint on a large, flat surface like a kitchen table; instead of sitting down, try standing up so you are looking down at your paper from a different angle. Put on some vibrant music to encourage you and try these exercises.

Choosing painting materials in your favourite colours is exciting and fun!

Fun with paint - Colour swirls

10-MINUTE EXERCISE Listen to the music you have put on, let sounds and rhythms fill you. Put a colour that appeals to you onto the brush and let it travel across the paper in a swirling path, maybe a wave pattern or a curling or spiralling effect. Clean the brush and take a different colour, maybe a contrast or something that attracts you, and repeat the same swirling movements. Change colour again a third time and watch how the curving patterns are covering the page. Do the colours meet? Do they run into each other? How do you like the shapes? Keep going until you feel you have enough colour on the page.

Fun with paint - Colour shapes

10-MINUTE EXERCISE On a fresh piece of paper, try painting 4 different coloured large shapes – a triangle, a circle, a square, a rectangle – and fill them in. When they are there in front of you, let your brush find a way of joining these shapes together, maybe a different coloured wavy line, maybe a series of dots, as you wish. Let your instinct guide you – there is no right or wrong, this is just a fun exploration of shape.

If you find you enjoy these exercises, keep on experimenting and let your love of colour guide you!

There is no end to the combinations of shape, colour and texture that you can create with paint. Relax completely, let yourself experiment and see what emerges on the paper!

sixth sense creative taste

Remember how taste is very much linked with smell? The aromas of foods are very responsible for how we react when we eat them, releasing a flood of digestive juices. In the busy rush of life it may be more convenient to reach for dinner from a box from the freezer, but when you have more time available your sense of taste can really be heightened by appreciating the aromas of cooking in anticipation of a wonderful meal.

Taste is also enhanced through the pleasure of sharing food. Many people live alone and tend to eat with the TV because instinctively we want company. Humans spent millennia hunting, gathering, cooking and sharing food communally. Dining alone is a modern trend, not just for single people; lifestyle demands may make eating together impractical on a daily basis. However, with a little effort and organization, meals can be prepared and shared and the experience becomes much more positive.

In Switzerland, especially at New Year, a traditional communal meal is the 'fondue savoyard', a dish of melted cheese, wine and garlic into which bread is dipped on the end of long forks. It is quick to make – if there are four of you, then share the preparation and it can be ready in less than 20 minutes! It is best made and served in a proper fondue set, with a ceramic pot and small burner, but you can use a heavy-bottomed saucepan instead. When the fondue is ready, you carry the bubbling pot to the table, where it sits on top of the burner, which needs to be on a low flame to keep the fondue warm. The fondue smells and tastes amazing – and eating it together from the pot in the centre of the table is a truly 'sharing' experience.

Eating meals around a central cooking pot is a tradition found in many cultures.

Use meal times to expand your senses of taste and smell – and celebrate with those you love.

Fondue Savoyard for Four People

2 large French bread sticks cut into 2 cm/1 inch cubes

400 g/1 lb Swiss Gruyère cheese, finely grated

225 g/½ lb Swiss Emmental cheese, finely grated

20 g/4 level teaspoons cornflour

300ml/10fl oz dry white wine

5 ml/1 teaspoon lemon juice

2 large cloves of garlic, cut into halves

15 ml/3 teaspoons kirsch (optional)

Sprinkle of black pepper

Sprinkle of freshly grated nutmeg

Rub the cooking pot with half a garlic clove. Put in the grated cheeses, cornflour, white wine and lemon juice and start it cooking on the hob over a very high heat, stirring constantly. The cheeses will form a large lump after about 5 minutes, but don't panic – keep stirring. In about another 5 minutes, the cheese melts and you have a bubbling sauce. Add the rest of the garlic, the kirsch and a sprinkle of black pepper and nutmeg. To eat the fondue, spear your bread chunks on long forks and dip into the pot, making sure you delve right to the bottom – you stir the fondue as it carries on cooking. If the fondue thickens, warm a wineglassful of dry white wine in a pan and add it to the sauce to thin it out. Enjoy!

sixth sense creative smell

Creating amazing aromas is the art of the perfumer. Top fragrances can contain hundreds of aromatic ingredients, all balanced to allow the scent to develop on warm skin and react with an individual's particular chemistry. Learning the art of perfumery takes many years, and top perfumers, called 'noses', are paid handsomely for their skills. Yet the fragrance of a rose, in all its delicate cool beauty with soft sweet undertones, cannot be totally reproduced by a perfumer, and rose perfumes will always be copies of something nature has perfected.

Floral essential oils are some of the most expensive – it takes approximately one hundred blossoms to give one drop of pure rose essential oil. Orange blossom flowers and jasmine flowers are also required in huge numbers and the amount of essential oil produced is tiny. Yet these exquisitely complex aromas are some of the finest and most beautiful available. They are complete perfumes in themselves; rubbed onto the skin, they release many different layers of fragrance – sweet, soft, citrusy, musky, rich and honey-like – we quickly run out of words to describe them.

Besides their extraordinary aromas, these oils have gentle but deep effects on mood. Orange blossom, soft and bitter-sweet, uplifts feelings of acute emotional stress. Rose – rich, sweet and honeyed – soothes feelings like grief and emotional pain. Jasmine – warm, musky and richly sweet – eases anxiety and deeply held tensions in mind and body.

Fortunately, these very expensive essential oils are available from good suppliers as blends – a few pure drops diluted in jojoba – so they can be obtained at a very reasonable cost.

ORANGE BLOSSOM

It takes hundreds of individual orange blossoms to create a bottle of essential oil, and the aroma is exquisite.

Deep relaxation – Scented-flower meditation

10-MINUTE EXERCISE You may wish to record this exercise on a tape.

To experience this deep floral relaxation, use Rose, Orange Blossom or Jasmine on your skin – put a tiny amount of blend behind your ears and on your wrists before you begin.

Sit back and relax in a warm, comfortable place, and begin to feel the aroma of your chosen flower drift over you. Breathe deeply and let your sense of smell begin to explore the richly complex fragrance, all the subtle notes and aspects in it. You may find your mind creates colour sensations for you, or you may see images unfold, or experience feelings in your body as you inhale the aroma. As you breathe in the scent around you, let go of stress and allow yourself to relax into a deeply contented state.

JASMINE

Creative smell 113

sixth sense creative touch

It is a very instinctive response to place a hand on someone when they are in pain or distress. The warmth and steadying presence of touch dissolves anxiety and fear, bringing calm and reassurance. Many cultures on the planet use their own traditional hands-on treatments where fingers and palms are used as skilful instruments, highly sensitive to minute changes in a person's temperature or areas in the body where there may be stress and tension. Massage is an excellent physical technique for easing out stress and tension, but so is the simple laying-on of hands.

When you place your hands on another person and leave them there for a few minutes, you may begin to feel changes – warmth, heat, perhaps a sensation of energy moving. The person receiving can focus on your hands and allow themselves to sink into a very deep state of relaxation where all the tension simply flows away. This type of simple touch works for children, adults or the elderly – for anyone who is open to receiving it. It requires no special tools, just respect from the giver and trust from the receiver. Animals respond particularly well to it – cats, for example, are supremely sensitive along their spines and will stretch out and purr at this touch.

To prepare for this session, make sure the room is warm and your friend can lie down comfortably on a mat on the floor, propped up on pillows and cushions, covered with a warm blanket. There is no need to undress. You need to sit or kneel beside them on whichever side is comfortable for you.

A quick and reassuring hug from a friend dissolves anxiety and restores a feeling of calm.

Laying on hands

10-MINUTE EXERCISE Sit comfortably beside your friend and place your hands across the tops of his or her shoulders, each side pointing in the same direction. Stay there for 2 minutes. Then move a little lower, to a level at the top of the chest, again for 2 minutes. Move lower, to the level of the stomach, again for 2 minutes.

Move down to the lower abdomen for 2 minutes. Finally, rest both hands over the tummy button for 2 minutes. When you have finished, allow your friend a little time to come slowly back into the room, then give him or her a glass of water.

It is interesting to ask your friend for feedback about this exercise – how did it feel, how relaxed did he or she become? Also share how you felt as the giver – perhaps you felt particular sensations in particular places. Giving and receiving this exercise is a very simple and nurturing experience, tuning your hands to new levels of sensitivity. It is also deeply relaxing and de-stressing at the end of a long day.

Make sure your partner is really warm and comfortable during this very relaxing exercise.

sixth sense creative sound

In China, Tibet and Nepal there is a tradition of using particular sound frequencies to achieve deep meditative states, which are thoroughly nourishing and replenishing to body and mind. These ancient sound techniques were being applied thousands of years ago; now, technology shows that these particular frequencies correspond amazingly to the vibratory rates of the brain. Sound affects structure – it can nourish or deplete depending on the intensity and the frequency; these ancient tones have been used for millennia to nourish and replenish human beings.

One of the instruments used is called a 'singing bowl'. These amazingly simple yet beautiful artefacts have a traditional use that goes back at least to 1000 BC; antique examples over four hundred years old can still be found. Modern bowls are still beautiful even though machinery is now used in the fabrication process, because the astonishing sounds arise through the combination of seven metals used to make them – gold, silver, mercury, copper, iron, tin and lead. In balance, melted together and hammered into shape, the metals combine to create a resonance chamber, so each bowl has a unique sound. Ancient Chinese beliefs linked the use of singing bowls to peace, harmony and long life.

Bowls can be bought from specialist instrument suppliers, and dealers in eastern artefacts; they will vary in price according to their age and size, from just several centimetres' diameter to over 40. The way to choose a bowl is to try them out. Each bowl is sold with a wooden beater, which is used to 'gong' the bowl, to bring it to life.

The sound of a singing bowl is astonishing – it seems like one note, then as you listen you will hear many other notes, called 'harmonics', which seem to echo around the main note. Allowing these sounds to bathe your ears is deeply relaxing to the mind.

Each Tibetan singing bowl has its own unique sound, created by the resonance of the metal chamber.

In countries in the East, sacred sound is seen as a bridge to spiritual awareness.

A sound bath with a singing bowl

 10-MINUTE EXERCISE To sound your bowl, place it on your left hand, holding your palm very flat. Strike the edge of the bowl gently with the beater, then start to run the beater around the very edge of the bowl, keeping a steady circular rhythm. In moments, the bowl starts to 'hum' and release its tones. Once the tone is steady, move the beater inside and feel the vibration of the bowl through your hand, as well as listening to the amazing sound. As it fades, start making circles again with the beater and the tone will return. Once you are used to playing the bowl, you can also place it on the base of a friend's spine, while they lie down and feel the sound moving around the body.

4 SensoryAwakening

By now, you will have realized that full sensory awakening totally changes your relationship with your environment, nature and the world you live in. Working with the senses to release stress, ease anxiety and open up creativity is a rich and rewarding way to enhance your life and the lives of those around you. So much stress arises through a state of numbness, which is not the way we humans are meant to live our lives. The world we live in is rich and vast, and we do not have to go far to begin to appreciate it in a different and more positive way. No matter where you are, you can begin; you can open yourself to a more colourful and varied experience of your world.

Awakening rejuvenation

As we said at the very beginning, some 'stress' is good for you. Positive stress is the kind of feeling that is generated when you are very happy, when you are enjoying what you are doing and you feel very fulfilled. If you are sunk in a very negative state, your energy will feel very sluggish, your interest in what surrounds you is limited, and your body processes are slow and cold. Getting in touch with your senses and waking them up brings warmth, interest and liveliness to your experience; you look further, you see further, you are inspired.

The more we expand into our external world, the more we learn about our internal world – this is an interesting balance. In the age we live in, spirituality is something that many people feel is not part of their daily life. Yet spirituality is simply this – balancing the inner and the outer. When there is balance there is no isolation, no anxiety or numbness – there is understanding, observation, inspiration. Many ancient traditions show that a sense of revival, rejuvenation and long life arise as a result of observing, understanding and enjoying our impressions of the world.

If you love colour, celebrate that in your living space, use gorgeous flowers to add vibrant tones and fragrance to your home. If you love to touch, take your hands into conscious contact with everything you meet, get your hands into the earth, mould clay, bake bread, give someone a nurturing hug. If sound moves you, open your voice, let your own individual note inspire you, or let music fill your ears and heart. Let the fragrances of the natural world all around you show you the changing seasons, from the cold quiet of winter to the warm aromas of summer; let your taste buds enjoy fruits and foods in season, full of colour, texture and aroma, even better when shared with people you love.

As Louis Armstrong sang, 'It's a wonderful world …' Try this simple exercise outside in the spring or summer, in your garden if you have one, or in a park, where you can really get close to a small area of nature.

Let each of your senses truly expand to shape and enhance your awareness of the world around you, in joy and appreciation of what you see, taste, smell, touch and hear.

Environment awareness

Find a quiet corner of your garden, or a park. Sit down comfortably on the ground, and stretch out your senses into what is around you. Feel what is under your hands, let your eyes really observe the hundreds of creatures living here – insects, birds and more – and also enjoy all of the colours and textures in the space; listen to the sounds, how many of them there are. Inhale deeply and let the smell and taste of the air fill your awareness. Now relax, deeply. Simply be part of this space.

Awakening the balancing act

As you now know, this book is full of ideas, exercises and ways you can use your senses to help you find a better sense of relaxation in your life. The beauty of all the suggestions is that they are all easy to do in about ten minutes. This makes any of the approaches available to you whenever you need, and many of them are easy to do at work or while on the move. The idea is that by starting to choose to spend ten-minute periods here and there doing sensory or creative things for yourself and other people, so gradually you will begin to build a new framework for yourself that will help you to relax, manage stress and ease anxiety.

As with all new things, it is easy to get over-enthusiastic and perhaps overwhelmed, then give up! It may be best to read through the whole book and then pick out areas that particularly appeal to you. Try one or two ideas first, concentrating on what is easy for you and fits with your individual lifestyle. Feel the effects, and notice the differences in your reactions. Then, if you wish, you can try a few more ideas. It takes patience to change the habits of a lifetime; your ten-minute 'time out' periods just need to unfold gently over a few months, and then you will really be able to assess how you are doing.

Be gentle with yourself – this is so important. There are no goals, no targets to meet; this is simply about you. It's a way to meet yourself again – maybe after a long while. If there is an aim, let it be quite simply that you enjoy what you are doing and experiencing. The more you enjoy it, the easier it will be for you to relax into it and let it nourish you.

One of the most exciting things about human life is that at every moment we can, if we so wish, choose to do something new. Even in the most challenging circumstances, something can shift – just the tiniest thing – and the whole picture changes. Just feeling a new sensation or trying a new experience can open up a new vision, a completely different way of seeing. This is how we move forward.

We have been given our magnificent senses as tools for life. They are with us in every moment, waking and asleep. They have been designed to let us appreciate all the wonders of the world we live in. Let them start working for you, and may your life simply expand and unfold, like a beautiful flower, in every way.

Let yourself find the inner peace, tranquillity and rest that will sustain you in your everyday life.

The landscape is an endless variety of glorious shapes and colours – spend time in nature and allow its elements to inspire and uplift you.

Resources and Information

Organizations

Alexander Technique
The Society of Teachers of the
Alexander Technique
20 London House
266 Fulham Road
London SW10 9EL
www.stat.org.uk

Aromatherapy
Aromatherapy Organizations
Council
3 Latymer Close
Braybooke
Market Harborough
Leics LE16 8LN
www.aoc.uk.net

Food and Health
The Institute for Optimum Nutrition
Blades Court
Deodar Road
London SW15 2NU
www.ion.ac.uk

Herbalism
National Institute of Medical
Herbalists
56 Longbrook Street
Exeter
Devon EX4 6AG
www.nmh.org.uk

Massage
British Massage Therapy Council
Greenbank House
65a Adelphi Street
Preston
Lancs PR1 7BH
www.bmtc.co.uk

Meditation
Acem School of Meditation
46 Lytton Road
Oxford
Oxon OX4 3PA
www.acem.com.uk

Pilates
The PILATESfoundation UK Limited
PO Box 19344
London W4 1GO
www.pilatesfoundation.com

Relaxation
Relaxation for Living Trust
12 New Street
Chipping Norton
Oxfordshire
OX7 5LJ
01983 868166

Yoga
British Wheel of Yoga
25 Jermyn Street
Sleaford
Lincs NG34 7RU
www.bwy.org.uk

Visualisation
UK Council for Psychotherapy
167-169 Great Portland Street
London WIN 5FB
www.psychotherapy.org.uk

Suppliers

Essential oils and carrier oils
Aromatherapy Products Ltd
(Tisserand)
Brighton BN3 7BA
Tel 01273 325666
www.tisserand.com

Essentially Oils Ltd
8–10 Mount Farm
Junction Road
Churchill
Chipping Norton
Oxfordshire OX7 6NP
Tel: 01608 659544
www.essentiallyoils.com

Instruments
Tibetan bowls
Earthsong: Angela McCarty
Tel 020 8941 2526
(Workshops for children, adults,
schools and special needs using
ethnic instruments)

Index